F. Carruthers Gould

Cartoons of the Campaign

A collection of political cartoons 1895

F. Carruthers Gould

Cartoons of the Campaign
A collection of political cartoons 1895

ISBN/EAN: 9783741195761

Manufactured in Europe, USA, Canada, Australia, Japa

Cover: Foto ©Andreas Hilbeck / pixelio.de

Manufactured and distributed by brebook publishing software
(www.brebook.com)

F. Carruthers Gould

Cartoons of the Campaign

THIRD EDITION.] [PRICE ONE SHILLING.

CARTOONS OF THE CAMPAIGN

BY

F. Carruthers Gould

1895

PUBLISHED BY

The "Westminster Gazette," Tudor Street, Blackfriars, E.C.

Cartoons of the Campaign

A COLLECTION OF POLITICAL CARTOONS

MADE DURING THE

General Election of 1895

BY

F. CARRUTHERS GOULD.

London:
THE "WESTMINSTER GAZETTE," TUDOR STREET, E.C.

1896.

The Drawings in this Volume appeared during the General Election of 1895 in "THE WESTMINSTER GAZETTE," "THE WESTMINSTER BUDGET," and "PICTURE POLITICS."

CONTENTS.

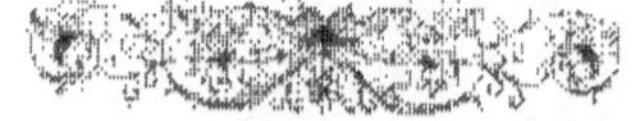

I.—EXIT SIR HENRY!

HOW THE TRICK WAS DONE. (*With apologies to Mr. Orchardson, R.A.*)

II.—THE GAME OF "MUSICAL CHAIRS."

WHO WILL BE SHELVED?

Everybody knows the game of "Musical Chairs." There are many players, but not seats enough for them all. The master of the ceremonies plays the music; and, when his playing ceases, those who can get seats, and those who can't are left out in the cold. Who will they be?

[WESTMINSTER GAZETTE, June 26.—The composition of the Administration was not at this time known. The [illegible] which appears to be [illegible] that Mr. Hanbury and Lord George Hamilton [illegible] chairs, and that Sir Edward Clarke and Mr. Courtney weren't playing.]

III.—PREPARING TO START.

IV.—BRINGING HIM UP TO DATE.

V.—THE SEAL FISHERY.

There was an old Marquis named Sarum,
Whose conduct was so harum-scarum,

He was rude to a seal; so head over heels
Went that clumsy old Marquis of Sarum.

[From Picture Politics.—Some misunderstanding was caused by the conduct of Lord Salisbury in writing his private secretary to Sir Henry Campbell-Bannerman, on the subject of the [illegible] of the Seals. Upon Lord Rosebery and Lord Kimberley calling attention to the matter in the House of Lords, Lord Salisbury apologised on June 18.]

VI.—"STEPPING-STONES."

"MEN MAY RISE ON STEPPING-STONES OF THEIR DEAD SELVES."

"I never thought that Lord Salisbury would have the slightest difficulty in forming a Government. There are plenty of candidates. Lord Salisbury has plenty of choice. There are members of this town who are ready at a moment's notice to undertake a Secretaryship of State to a Lordship-in-Waiting."
Mr. CHAMBERLAIN, at Holloway, *June* 17, 1885.

[WESTMINSTER GAZETTE, *June* 27.—It was announced that Mr. Chamberlain had accepted a Secretaryship of State in Lord Salisbury's Government.]

VII.—"IN THE WAY HE SHOULD WALK."

SCHOOLMASTER S-L-SB-RY: "Now, my boy, what have you got there?"

MASTER J. CH-MB-RL-N: "Please, sir, I didn't mean it; I won't ever say it again."

SCHOOLMASTER: "You used to talk about 'ransom.' What did you mean by it?"

SCHOOLBOY: Please, sir, that was a long time ago, and I am very willing to confess that the word was not very well chosen to express my meaning." [See speech at Birmingham, November 18, 1891.]

SCHOOLMASTER: "You said that I was the spokesman of a class who toil not neither do they spin. What did you mean by that?"

SCHOOLBOY: "That was in my Radical days. I have since explained that I am proud of being allied with the gentlemen of England, and that I am ready to defend the House of Lords against all attacks."

SCHOOLMASTER (laying down the birch): "Good boy! You shall have a prize."

[WESTMINSTER GAZETTE, *July* 1.]

VIII.—THE TABLES TURNED.

SCHOOLMASTER: "Now, Sir, what have you got there? How dare you?"

SCHOOLBOY: "Please, sir, it's only an old exercise; I wrote it last term—'in your Radical days.'"

SCHOOLMASTER: "Those days, my child, are over, never to return. 'Other times, other manners.' Now, say your new exercise."

SCHOOLBOY: "I am in favour of Mr. Chamberlain's schemes; but (*sotto voce*) I don't believe in them a bit."

SCHOOLMASTER (*interrupting*): "What's that, sir?"

SCHOOLBOY (*humbly*): "Please, sir, nothing, sir."

SCHOOLMASTER (*sternly*): "You had better be careful, sir; remember that I shall tolerate no impertinence.

[WESTMINSTER GAZETTE, *July* 12.]

IX.—PITY THE POOR DUMB!

THE ATTITUDE OF THE NEW MINISTRY.

LORD SALISBURY (House of Lords, *June* 27): "We have but one policy, and that is, Dissolution."

MR BALFOUR (Manchester, *June* 26): "Our policy can be expressed in a single word—'Dissolution.'"

SIR MICHAEL HICKS-BEACH (Bristol, *July* 1): "What was to be their policy? (Cheers.) He must not go too far in that." (Laughter.)

[WESTMINSTER GAZETTE, *July* 2.]

X.—DOCTORING THE OLD HORSE.

UNCLE S-L-SB-RY: "There! that's first rate; he's swallowed it."

NEPHEW B-LF-R: "Yes; but he looks awfully sick over it. Hadn't we better let him rest a day or two before we try these boluses?"

See leading article in the Times newspaper, June 27:—

"It must be regarded as an advantage rather than otherwise that no further Ministerial appointments are announced this morning. . . . An interval of a couple of days will afford an opportunity for the constituencies to arrange their ideas and to recover from the somewhat bewildering effect of rapid changes. . . . Lord Salisbury and Mr. Balfour have secured, as partners in the work of administration, the Duke of Devonshire and Mr. Chamberlain. . . . The new and more intimate relations established by the acceptance, on the part of the Liberal Unionist leaders, of formal responsibility for the policy of the Unionist Party may profitably receive for a day or two the undistracted attention of the electorate."

[WESTMINSTER GAZETTE, *July* 3.—The Tory Party was, however, [illegible] the [illegible] Bolus; but it had plenty of others to swallow, as a later cartoon shows.]

XI.—ON THE ALTAR OF THE COALITION.

(From Picture Politics.)

XII.—DESIGN FOR A WEATHERCOCK.

[From Picture Politics.]

XIII.—HIS LAST GARMENT.

"Come out of it!"
"I can't: it's the only thing I've got left."

[From Picture Politics.]

XIV.—THE FAMILY 'BUS.

CONDUCTOR OF THE MINISTERIAL OMNIBUS: "I am afraid, ma'am, there isn't room inside for all of you. How many of you are there?"

PASSENGER: "There's only me, and my little boy, and this kind gentleman (Mr. P..w..ll W..ll..ms), and my little dog. You really must make room, Mr. Conductor; some of the gentlemen must get outside."

[WESTMINSTER GAZETTE, *July* 4.—The following appointments had been announced:—

Mr. Jesse Collings: Under Secretary, Home Office.
Mr. Powell Williams: Financial Secretary, War Office.
Mr. Austen Chamberlain: Civil Lord, Admiralty.]

XV.—THE FAMILY PIE.

"You look after your family. I'll look after mine."

XVI.—UNIONIST GEOGRAPHY.

PROFESSOR SALISBURY GIVES A DEMONSTRATION IN THE NEW SEPARATION: "Here, gentlemen, is a map of the United Kingdom, brought up to date in harmony with Unionist principles. You will kindly cross out Scotland, and Wales, and all Ireland except Ulster. They don't count. England we leave in, in virtue of the Southern part of it, which gives us a majority. This, you perceive, is the way to make a United Kingdom."

The following extracts from Lord Salisbury's speeches were subjoined: "By the working of the Constitution the House of Lords represents the overwhelming opinion of England, and almost the unanimous opinion of the Loyalists of Ireland, and is overborne by the other parts of Ireland and by the *Celtic fringe* which surrounds the western side of Great Britain. Do you imagine that, so long as England and Ulster retain their present views, the House of Lords is likely to be frightened?"—Lord SALISBURY, at Belfast, May 24, 1893.

"The present Government say they cannot get the measures they desire passed. Well, they know perfectly well why that is. They know that the House of Lords represents an overwhelming majority of England in its objections to those measures, and it is only by a very scanty majority, *made up from various other places*—especially from the south and west of Ireland—that the noble lord is able to carry his measures through the House of Commons."—Lord SALISBURY in the House of Lords, Feb. 5, 1895.]

[WESTMINSTER GAZETTE, *July* 6.]

XVII.—KING SALISBURY AND THE PEOPLE.

His Majesty awaiting the results of the Elections: "What does it matter? If we win, well and good. If we lose, haven't I got my [illegible] for the maniacs?"

[From PICTURE POLITICS. See Lord Salisbury's speech in the House of Lords, July 6, [illegible]:—"The country has been saved by the [illegible] that the House of Lords has imposed on the Radical Party. If they complain of [illegible], my reply is that as soon as they take their own clothes and are in their right minds they will not find the [illegible] embarrassing." A further illustration of Lord Salisbury's theory is given on the next page.]

XVIII.—"MANACLES FOR MANIACS."

SIR W. HARCOURT.

MR. ASQUITH.

MR. JOHN MORLEY.

SIR H. FOWLER.

MR. ACLAND.

SIR H. CAMPBELL-BANNERMAN.

[From Picture Politics

XIX.—IN THE PROPERTY ROOM.

THE TORY POLICY FOR IRELAND.

(*Mr. Arthur Balfour showing Mr. Gerald round his Coercionist Museum and Picture Gallery.*)

Mr. Balfour, asked in the House of Commons, on July 6, to declare his Irish policy, said:—"We shall hold to the opinions we have always held." But added, "We cannot be expected to make a declaration of Government policy just now."

The fact is, as Mr. Acland said at Hammersmith, that "the members of the new company had been conducting their rehearsals in private, and the public had not yet been admitted to see the play."

Our picture gives a strictly private view of the Irish property room.

[Westminster Gazette, *July* 8.]

XX.—JUGGLER JOE AND HIS VANISHING PROGRAMME.

JUGGLER: "I will now proceed, ladies and gentlemen, to roll up this extensive programme into a ball, and the Old Party will swallow it without the slightest difficulty."

OLD PARTY: "Look here! I say! I'm not going to swallow all that!"

JUGGLER (*aside*): "All right, my lord! You sit tight. You've only got to *pretend*. I'll manage all the vanishing business."

[WESTMINSTER GAZETTE, *July* 9.]

XXI.—DRESSING THE SHOP WINDOW.

SHOPWALKER S-L-SB-RY: "Don't crowd the window, Joseph!"

SHOP-ASSISTANT CH-MB-RL--N: "All right, my lord! You leave it to me."

["The shutters were still up, and the partners in the new concern were apparently engaged in the operation of dressing the shop window. (Renewed laughter.) But on Monday morning they would have to open for business, and he would [illegible] that the great bulk of the stock would be found to consist of [illegible] goods. (More laughter and cheers.)" Mr. ASQUITH, at Ashton-under-Lyne, July 6, 1895.]

[From PICTURE POLITICS.]

XXII. COCK-A-DOODLE-DOO!

"Lord Charles Beresford has retired, as others before him retired, before the wrath of Mr. Chamberlain. The dictator of Birmingham allows no rival near the throne. He prefers to remain cock of his own walk."—(*Daily Paper*.)

XXIII.—"WHICH IS LEADING WHICH?"

JOHN BULL to PORTER B[illegible]: "Where are you taking him?"
PORTER: "I ain't taking him anywhere."
JOHN BULL: "Well, then, where's he taking you?"
PORTER (*indignantly*): "He ain't taking me."
JOHN BULL: "Then, where *is* he going?"
PORTER: "I don't know. He's eaten all his direction labels."

[The *Spectator*, referring to the above cartoon, says:—"That is laying emphasis on Mr. Chamberlain's greatest achievement. He has eaten all his labels."—*July* [illegible].]

[WESTMINSTER GAZETTE, *July* [illegible].]

XXIV.—"WHICH SWALLOWED THE OTHER?"

Several Liberal speakers have, in reference to the coalition between Lord Salisbury and Mr. Chamberlain, recited the verses :—

There was an Old Party of Niger
Who smiled as he rode on a tiger;
They finished the ride with that Party inside
And the smile on the face of the tiger.

"But the question is," said Mr. Chamberlain, "which has swallowed the other?"

Our artist gives what he takes to be Mr. Chamberlain's answer. But we daresay Lord Salisbury's is very different.

[Westminster Gazette, *July 15*.]

XXV.—THE TORY VILLAGE.

A TOY FOR LITTLE TORIES.

[From Picture Politics.]

XXVI.—"WHAT IT MAY COME TO."

A SUGGESTION FOR THE CHRISTMAS PANTOMIME.

"Now then, join up for our performance in the Great Coalition Show."
"Confound the fellow! I suppose I must, but I do believe I could have gone on without the hind legs after all!"

[Westminster Gazette, *July 17.*]

XXVII.—ALMOST TOO MUCH OF A GOOD THING.

More gains! Why, confound it! I could have done without that fellow after all!

More gains! Why, confound it! That fellow will be wanting to do without me after all!

[Westminster Gazette, July [illegible].]

XXVIII.—TRAVELLING FOR THE NEW FIRM.

Yes, my name is Joe Wellington Wells,
I travel in Unionist spells;
I've got a selection, defying detection,
Of the newest political sells

[From Picture Politics.]

XXIX.—"ATTEND TO YOUR MARKETS!"

"How about those Social Programmes, sir? Hadn't I better be getting on with some of them?"

"Don't bother me! Mind your own business! Is not your own department enough to keep you out of mischief? Why can't you attend to your markets?"

[See *Times* leading article, *July* 1]: "Mr. Balfour will bear the chief share in the burden of introducing, defending, and piloting through the House all the measures of national reform, &c., &c. . . . . . Mr. Chamberlain will have very large and important duties at the Colonial Office . . . . . promoting the opening up of new markets."]

[WESTMINSTER GAZETTE, *July* 16.]

XXXI.—"THE LITTLE VULGAR BOY" IN POLITICS.

[Westminster Gazette, July 5. At a previous Election Lord Salisbury had compared the Irish to Hottentots, and had expressed his astonishment at any constituency electing "a black man"—i.e., a native of India. The return of "a black man" as a supporter of Lord Salisbury was one of the incidents of the present Election.]

XXX.—THE THREE STAGES OF A SALISBURY BLAZER.

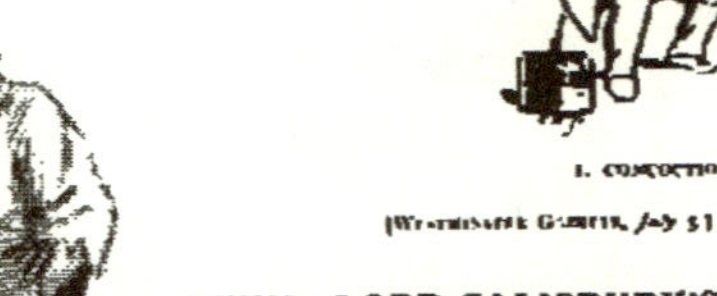

1. CONCOCTION. 2. DEFEAT. 3. INJURED INNOCENCE.

[Westminster Gazette, July 5.]

XXXII.—LORD SALISBURY'S BLACK BABY.

XXXIII.—PARTNERS.

To Deputation: "My partner {Mr. Chamberlain / Lord Salisbury} looks after that department. You had better apply to him. Oh! you have seen him, and he sent you to me. Then you had better leave it and call again."

[Westminster Gazette, July 15.]

XXXIV.—"GOOD-BYE, GERALD!"

ARTHUR (*loquitur*): "Good-bye, Gerald! Cheer up! You'll do very well in Ireland. A sympathetic manner and a sense of humour are all the Irish ever want."

[WESTMINSTER GAZETTE, *July* 6.]

XXXV.—THE ATTITUDE OF THE INDEPENDENT LABOUR PARTY.

MR. K— H—: "Can't get in myself, but I can keep a few others out anyway."

[WESTMINSTER GAZETTE, *July* 17.]

XXXVI.—"THE SPECIAL PLEADER IN POLITICS."

"Heavens and earth! I've taken up the wrong brief. Lucky I found it out in time! It would have been deuced awkward if I'd gone into Court with it."

[*See* leading article in the WESTMINSTER GAZETTE, *July* [illegible]:—

The truth is that Mr. CHAMBERLAIN is the supreme special pleader in politics. There never was any one to equal him in that respect, and as he grows older he seems to surpass himself. He has supplied a complete set of arguments for almost every point of view in politics—for Home Rule and against Home Rule; for ending the House of Lords and for leaving it in possession; [illegible] and for [illegible] those who attempt to disestablish them. He has denounced Toryism from a Radical point of view, and Radicalism from a Tory point of view; he has taken every prominent statesman in detail—Mr. GLADSTONE, Lord HARTINGTON, the Duke of [illegible], Mr. GOSCHEN, and [illegible] shown us first their [illegible] and then their [illegible] side, or the reverse. The great [illegible] which were ten years ago to inspire the democracy and lead them into their promised land, are now, according to the same authority, the [illegible] of [illegible] minds.]

[WESTMINSTER GAZETTE, *July* 22.]

XXXVII.—THE UNION.

"UNITED WE STAND, DIVIDED WE FALL."

[Westminster Gazette, July 18.]

XXXVIII.—THE PHARISEE AND THE PUBLICAN.

"Well, I never! and him so friendly when the elections was on! Talk about vested interests, indeed! Why now we've won a glorious victory together, he don't know me! That's a nice way to treat a pal."

[See letter from a well-known clergyman in the *Times*, July 27: "Will you allow me to say a word . . . in connexion with the elections, now nearly completed, in respect to the cause of Temperance? . . . I cannot but feel that in several quarters in the present elections it may have been, and is being, made by the Unionist side of the cry not to 'rob the poor man of his beer,' which is very demoralising. Such an appeal to the love of beer is degrading. . . . As the great majority of Churchmen have felt themselves constrained to support the same political party [as the brewers], they appear to be under a special obligation to take care that the cause of Temperance may not be allowed to suffer."]

[Westminster Gazette, *August 3*.]

XXXIX.—"A GOOD STORY"

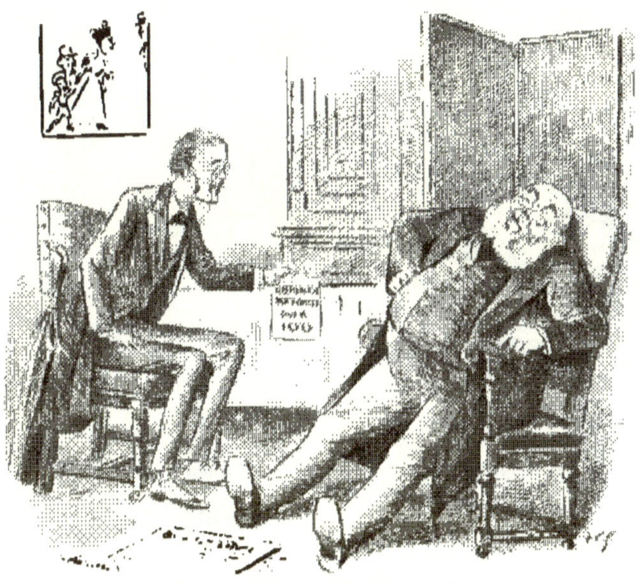

(*With apologies to Leo Hermann.*)

UNCLE: "Good boy, Arthur! How did you manage it?"
NEPHEW: "The old game, uncle! I pledged you to nothing, but we promised them everything."
UNCLE: "Clever boy!"

[WESTMINSTER GAZETTE, *July* [illegible].]

XL.—"WHAT WILL HE DO WITH IT?"

"Yes, he's a good big one, but how am I going to feed him?"

[Westminster Gazette, *July* 13.]

XLI.—BOWERS OF BLISS IN THE COALITION TEA-GARDENS.

"They are still in the honeymoon."—Lord Rosebery at the Albert Hall.

[Mr. Chamberlain and Lord Salisbury.]
"Do you know, Marquis dear, I always did love you Tories?"

[Mr. Collings and Mr. Chaplin.]
"Come live with me, my Jesse, and be my love, and we will all the pleasures prove—of three acres and a cow."

[Mr. Courtney and Mr. A. Chamberlain.]
"And she'll come for a little [illegible] 'skeleton,' won't she?"

[Sir Henry James and Lord Halsbury.]
"Well, you don't find this Tory drink so bad after all, old boy, do you?"

[Westminster Gazette, July 14.]

XLII.—"ANYTHING TO OBLIGE!"

MR. G.: "I hope you will quite understand that my speech is for the sole purpose of giving you a friendly lead."
LORD SALISBURY: "H'm! (hesitating) Really I hardly like to trouble you."
MR. G.: "Oh, no trouble, I assure you! Anything to oblige."

[In yesterday's *Times*:—" Mr. Gladstone has hitherto steadily refused to speak in public on the Armenian question, lest his doing so might injure the cause by giving occasion to turn it into a party question. The effect of the meeting will doubtless be to strengthen Lord Salisbury's hands. It can hardly fail to emphasise the fact that Lord Salisbury has the British nation at his back in insisting on effectual security for the better government of Armenia."]

[WESTMINSTER GAZETTE, *August* 1.—Mr. Gladstone had arranged to address a public meeting on the Turkish Atrocities in Armenia.]

XLIII.—"THE POLICY OF THE SNOOZE."

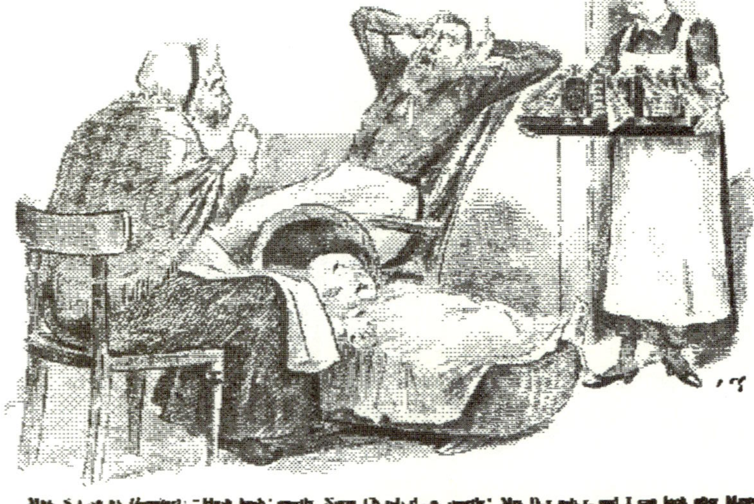

Mrs. S[illegible] ([illegible]): "Hush, hush! quietly, Nurse Ch[illegible], quietly! Mrs. D[illegible] and I can look after Master John Bull very nicely, thank you. Put the medicines down, and we'll think about giving him a very small dose presently. But the great thing is to keep him asleep."

[Westminster Gazette, July 11.]

XLIV.—SUGGESTED TO TORY HOUSEHOLDERS.

"Confound that bird! I must cure him of that crowing!"

"That'll keep him quiet!"

[Westminster Gazette, July 27.]

XLV.—THE POOR MAN AND HIS PEER.

"One remarkable feature of the elections has been the rally of the working classes to the House of Lords. Beer has had nothing to do with it."—*Tory paper.*

In fact, there can be no doubt that our familiar figure of the Tory sandwich man will now have to be brought up to date by the substitution, as above, of a *P* for a *B*.

(Westminster Gazette, *July* 31.)

XLVI.—"FUSION."

JOSEPH AS THE NEW BENJAMIN.

["As Mr. Chamberlain is now a member of the (Tory) Cabinet, he will not, on the eve of the meeting of Parliament, issue a separate circular to his followers in the House of Commons."—*Standard*, this morning.]

[WESTMINSTER GAZETTE, *August* 1.]

XLVII.—THE LIBERAL WRECK.

OLD PILOT: "I wonder if I could have saved her."

[WESTMINSTER GAZETTE, *July* [illegible].]

XLVIII.—THE GREAT COMET OF 1895.

"The general features of a comet are a definite point or nucleus, and a train following the nucleus. The name 'tail' is given to the appendage. The movements of planets are often from east to west, or retrograde. The orbits of comets present every variety of eccentricity."—*Encyclopædia.*

[Westminster Gazette, July 31.]

Do these Cartoons Amuse you? If so, you should Subscribe at once to

PICTURE POLITICS

The Penny Pictorial Monthly, of Political Powder and Shot, for Political Associations, Parliamentary Candidates, Electors, and all persons interested in the Work and Warfare of Politics of To-day.

Illustrated by MR. F. C. GOULD.

LORD SALISBURY ON THE SITUATION.

POLITICS, said Lord Salisbury in speech on the situation the other day, "politics are for the moment terribly dull."

"POLITICS ARE DULL."

Lord Salisbury, we do not doubt, correctly gauged the situation on the facts before him.

But he made one great mistake. He had forgotten to read PICTURE-POLITICS. He has remedied his mistake, we are sure, by this time.

"BUT 'PICTURE-POLITICS' ARE NOT!"

PICTURE-POLITICS is Full of Points,
Full of Pictures,
Full of Faces;

And, at last! politics are made pleasant.

"Reading," says Bacon, "maketh a full man, conference a ready man, and writing an exact man."

Read PICTURE-POLITICS, and you will be full of useful facts. Buy it and keep it; read and digest it; and you will be an up-to-date politician.

PICTURE-POLITICS shows the month's political record at a glance.

The humours of Parliament and the amusing side of political controversies are depicted month by month by the popular pencil of F. C. Gould.

Members, candidates, and all fighting politicians will find in PICTURE-POLITICS an unfailing supply of Powder and Shot.

Some men say that politics are dull. This is because they have not yet seen PICTURE-POLITICS.

Some women say they cannot bear politics. "Oh! those horrid politics." But take PICTURE-POLITICS home with you, leave it lying on the table, and they will be converted.

Give a copy of PICTURE-POLITICS to your son. He may become a Pitt some day. Who knows? And the youth of one generation are the electors of the next.

Do not forget the daughters. They will be the "Liberal Women" or Primrose Dames of the future. Influence is as important as votes.

MR. GLADSTONE'S READING.

It may be taken as granted that the first use to which Mr. Gladstone put his recovered eyesight after the operation was to read PICTURE-POLITICS:—

And the political world need not have been puzzled to know why Sir William Harcourt retired to his country house the other day. Of course, it was to enjoy a quiet reading of PICTURE-POLITICS:—

Price One Penny Monthly; by Post Eighteenpence a Year. N.B.—Special Terms for Large Quantities. There is no more effective method of Political Education than the distribution of "Picture-Politics."

PICTURE POLITICS *is obtainable at any Bookseller's, Newsagent's, at the Railway Bookstalls, or from the Publisher.*

Published at THE WESTMINSTER GAZETTE and WESTMINSTER BUDGET Offices, Tudor Street, London, E.C.

HOLLOWAY'S

PILLS AND OINTMENT

Have proved a blessing wherever introduced, and for all Complaints it has been impossible to find their equal.

THE PILLS REGULATE DIGESTION

and cure all disorders of the Liver; they are invaluable for Female Ailments.

THE OINTMENT CURES SKIN AFFECTIONS

of every kind, such as

Eczema, Scurvy, Pimples, Blotches, Ringworm, Ulcerations, &c.

Manufactured only at 78, NEW OXFORD STREET, LONDON; sold by all Chemists and Medicine Vendors.

HARRISON AND SONS, PRINTERS IN ORDINARY TO HER MAJESTY, ST. MARTIN'S LANE, LONDON

ADVERTISEMENTS.

JAEGER

PURE WOOL UNDERWEAR, HOSIERY, PYJAMAS, RUGS, BLANKETS, DRESSING GOWNS, SHAWLS, CORSETS, BOOTS AND SHOES, &c., &c.

TRADE MARK ON EACH GARMENT.

The Best is the Cheapest!
Fixed moderate prices for first quality.

PERMANENT PROTECTION FROM CHILL.

JAEGER DEPOTS:—
3 and 4, PRINCES STREET, CAVENDISH SQUARE (near Regent Circus).
126, REGENT STREET (near the Quadrant).
30, SLOANE STREET (adjoining McPherson's Gymnasium).
456, STRAND (near Trafalgar Square).
85 and 86, CHEAPSIDE (near King Street).

TAILORING:—
42, CONDUIT STREET, NEW BOND STREET, W.

Dr. Jaeger's "Health Culture," 188 pp., and Illustrated Jaeger Price List, sent free.

THE JAEGER GOODS ARE SOLD IN MANY TOWNS.

Address sent from the JAEGER CO.'S Head Office,
95, MILTON STREET, LONDON, E.C.

 ### DO YOU ADMIRE SPORT?
DO YOU KNOW LONDON?

SHORTLY.
THE
SPORTFOLIO.
Portraits and Biographies of the Heroes and Heroines of Sport and Pastime.

TO BE COMPLETED IN TWELVE 6d. PARTS. POST FREE, 8d. EACH.

SHORTLY.
ROUND LONDON.
An Album of Pictures from Photographs of the Famous Streets, Remarkable Features and Buildings, and Beautiful Spots in and around the Metropolis.

TO BE COMPLETED IN TWELVE 6d. PARTS. POST FREE, 8d. each.

Handsome Portfolio Cases for Holding the 12 loose parts of any of the four Albums. Price 2s. 6d. Handsome Cloth Covers for binding up the 12 parts. Price 2s.

MAY BE OBTAINED TO ORDER FROM ANY BOOKSELLER, NEWSAGENT, OR RAILWAY BOOKSTALL.

GEORGE NEWNES, LTD., 8, 9, 10, 11, SOUTHAMPTON STREET, STRAND, LONDON, W.C.

ADVERTISEMENTS.

FIVE PER CENT. DEBENTURE,
WITH GUARANTEED PROGRESSIVE BONUS.
EVERY CONTINGENCY PROVIDED FOR.
ILLUSTRATION AT AGE 35.

Debenture, **£1,000**. Annual Deposit, **£43 4s. 0d.** (limited to 20 Years).

GUARANTEES IN CASE OF DEATH.

If Death occur during	A – Payable to Beneficiary immediately on Proof of Death.	B – Annuity for 20 years following death of Insured, which Principal at end of 20 Years or at Death of Beneficiary, if prior.		C – If Beneficiary flows 20 Years Company will have paid	D – Total Amount Paid for same.
		Annuity.	Principal.		
1st Year	£25	£50	1000	£2025	£43 4 0
5th Year	125	50	1000	2125	216 0 0
10th Year	250	50	1000	2250	432 0 0
15th Year	375	50	1000	2375	648 0 0
20th Year	500	50	1000	2500	864 0 0

The amounts in Column A are applicable for Death Duties, &c.; the Annuity (Column B) for Children's Education, &c., and the Principal for Marriage Settlement, or Start in Business or Profession.

GUARANTEES IN CASE OF DISCONTINUANCE.

On legal surrender of the Debenture, after payment of three or more full years' deposits, the Company will issue a Paid-up Policy for a specified amount, payable immediately upon proof of the death of the Insured.

After Years' Deposit Paid.	Paid-up Policy.	Total Amount Paid for Same.
5	£168 10 0	£216 0 0
10	282 10 0	432 0 0
15	585 0 0	648 0 0
20	947 10 0	864 0 0

OPTIONS AT THE END OF 20 YEARS.

This form of contract is new and original in its essential features. Under it the Debenture-holder has several options of settlement, or continuance, as below stated. The cash and equivalent values include the legal reserve, the amount of which is specifically guaranteed, and the surplus. What this surplus will be in future settlements will necessarily depend upon subsequent experience. The surplus incorporated with the cash value or equivalent options in this example is to be understood as an adopted illustration based upon actual experience in policy settlements of recent date.

A	**£1,146 IN CASH.** Reserve and Earned Surplus.	**"A"** To surrender the Debenture by withdrawing in cash, the guaranteed reserve, and the accumulated surplus that may be apportioned.
B	**£1,828 DEBENTURE AT DEATH.** Bearing 4 per cent. Interest, = £91 8s. 0d.	**OR, "B"** To add the insurance value of accumulated surplus in the amount of the original Debenture, such additions carrying the 4 per cent. bonus in the dividends, and continue the combined amounts, participating in future bonuses. **NO MORE DEPOSITS.**
C	**£550 8s. 2d.** Cash Surplus at £48 14s. 1d. Equivalent Life Income of **£1,000 DEBENTURE AT DEATH,** Bearing 4 per cent. Interest.	**OR, "C"** To draw accumulated surplus in cash, or as an equivalent life income, and continue Debenture, participating in future bonuses. **NO MORE DEPOSITS.**

THIS INVESTMENT CAN ONLY BE MADE WITH THE
MUTUAL LIFE INSURANCE COMPANY OF NEW YORK.
IN FIFTY-TWO YEARS THE COMPANY HAS

		Amount
1.	Paid to the Beneficiaries of DECEASED MEMBERS	£93,568,40 13 4
2.	Paid to Living MEMBERS, for Matured Endowments, Annuities, Surrender Values and Bonuses	46,923,437 5 10
3.	Balance of Income Accumulated for paying Claims and Bonuses	41,300,326 10 3
	Total Benefits to Policyholders	**£181,792,273 8 5**

A GOOD RECORD IS THE BEST GUARANTEE FOR THE FUTURE.

The Company has no Shareholders, and all the Profits belong to its Policyholders.
Full particulars of the various Policies issued by the Company may be had upon application to the

Head Office for the United Kingdom,
17 and 18, CORNHILL, LONDON, E.C.,
D. C. HALDEMAN, *General Manager.*

PRICE ONE SHILLING.

THE WESTMINSTER CARTOONS

No 2

1896

BY

F. Carruthers Gould

PUBLISHED BY

NEW BRANCH: 21, HIGH STREET, KENSINGTON, W.

THE SIMPSON LEVER CHAIN
The Greatest Cycling Invention of the Age.
No More Toiling up Hills Against the Wind. Ladies can use Shorter Cranks with Ease.

IT HOLDS ALL
THE BEST
PATH RECORDS.

IT IS USED
BY ALL THE BEST
RACING MEN.

IT WINS ALL THE
IMPORTANT RACES.

IT HOLDS THE
London to York Record :
ALSO THE
BORDEAUX to PARIS
RECORD,
AND
THE WORLD'S HOUR
RECORD
Of 30 Miles, 214 Yards,
BY TOM LINTON.

THE SIMPSON CYCLES ARE ALL FITTED WITH THE SIMPSON CHAIN,
AND ARE HIGHEST SPECIMENS OF THE CYCLE BUILDING ART.

London Show Rooms: 119, REGENT STREET, W.

THE

Westminster Cartoons

The Originals of several of the Drawings in this and in the previous issue of Political Cartoons can be purchased on application to the Assistant Editor "Westminster Gazette" Office,
Tudor Street.

895

F. CARRUTHERS GOULD.

London:
THE "WESTMINSTER GAZETTE," TUDOR STREET, E.C.
1896.

PREFACE.

The Cartoons and Drawings in this Volume appeared in the "Westminster Gazette," the "Westminster Budget," and "Picture Politics."

Although not arranged in strict chronological sequence, they cover all the matters of political interest since the General Election of 1895.

The earlier Cartoons deal with political events connected directly with The House of Commons. Then the passing cloud of difficulty with the United States, the Ashanti Expedition, and the attitude of Great Britain towards the Sultan of Turkey and the Eastern Question, are illustrated.

Next come the South African Questions and the difficulties with the Transvaal, in which Mr. Chamberlain figures in various forms. Then the Soudan Question is treated in its different phases, and last comes the Education Bill, bringing the series up to a recent date.

CONTENTS.

I.—THE NEW AUNT SALLY IN THE COMMONS.

1. Mr. Walter Long. 3. Lord G. Hamilton. 5. Mr. Goschen. 7. Mr. Chamberlain. 8. Sir M. Hicks-Beach.
2. Mr. Gerald Balfour. 4. Mr. Ritchie. 6. Mr. Balfour. 9. Sir M. W. Ridley. 10. Mr. Chaplin.

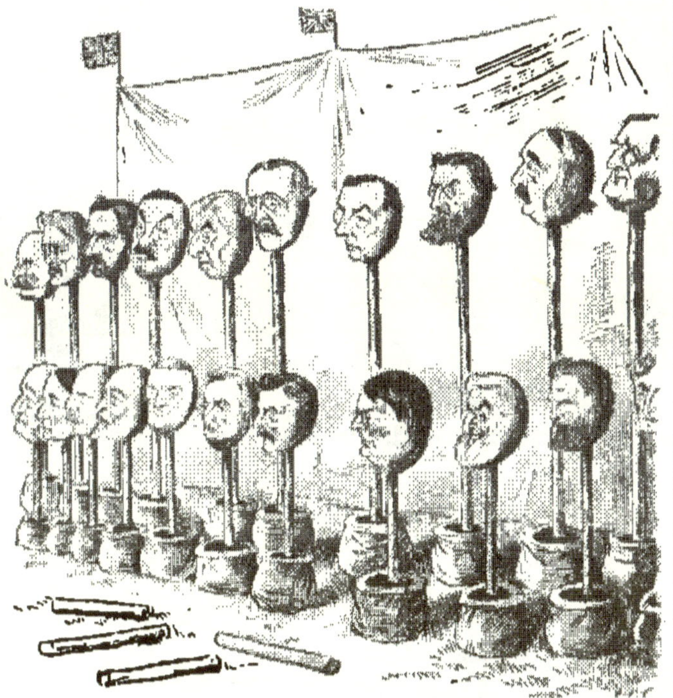

1. Sir R. Webster. 3. Mr. Macartney. 5. Mr. Austen Chamberlain. 7. Mr. Brodrick. 9. Mr. Jesse Collings.
2. Mr. G. Curzon. 4. Sir J. Gorst. 6. Mr. P. Williams. 8. Mr. Hanbury. 10. Mr. T. W. Russell.
11. Sir C. Pearson.

The Parliamentary machine is getting into working order, and the new Ministers have entered upon their daily task of answering questions. [illegible]

(Westminster Gazette, August [illegible].)

II. MORE BOWERS OF BLISS.

"Do you *really* love me, Gerald?"
(GERALD: "I—I—I'm trying to."

"Yes! Matthew, we are yours!"
SIR MATTHEW: "But look here—I say—I haven't promised.
(*Aside*: "I hope to goodness I haven't committed myself.")

During last Session Mr. Gerald Balfour expressed a hope that he might [illegible] the [illegible] of the [illegible], and Sir Matthew White Ridley promised to keep an open mind on Mr. [illegible] Redmond's appeal for the release of the dynamiters.

WESTMINSTER GAZETTE, August [illegible].

III.—A TIFF.

"NEVER AGAIN!" (MR. J. REDMOND AND MR. GERALD BALFOUR.)

WESTMINSTER GAZETTE, February [illegible].

IV.—THE COLD WATER CURE

The Duke of Devonshire: "Wretched little things! There's nothing like cold water for them."—(*Vide* recent speeches.)

Parliament has not been sitting this month, and Ministers have apparently been taking holiday. But one and all have been most [illegible] engaged upon their holiday task, which consists in whittling away, or explaining away, the [illegible] promises which were made at the last election. Mr. Balfour made a beginning by [illegible], then Lord George Hamilton followed [illegible]. [illegible] on September [illegible] the Duke of Devonshire made a speech in which he told the farmers to expect little or nothing. [illegible] by telling the landlords that they must expect nothing more than the farmers. Then finally, on the [illegible], the Duke of Devonshire made another speech, [illegible] Old Age Pensions. [illegible] the Duke in the act of drowning the Tory kittens, to the great satisfaction of the Tory cat.

Westminster Gazette, September [illegible].

V.—THE HOT AND COLD GOVERNMENT.

(It is understood that a bath-room is being fitted up at Downing-street for the reception of deputations.)

[illegible]

Westminster Gazette, November [illegible]

VI.—THE COLD WATER TAP AGAIN

The cold water tap was full on Friday, Feb. 8, when Lord Salisbury received the Bishop of London and a deputation from the Church of England Temperance Society. The Bishop and his friends returned in a drenched condition, and reported that they had got nothing. The Bishop endeavoured to be cheerful, and said:—"So far from allowing ourselves to be stopped because we have come for a moment to a stone wall we are bound to see whether we cannot take down that stone wall."

VII.—"SCOTCH."

BARMAID: "Irish, sir?"

JOHNNY: "No, my dear, I think I'll try a drop of Scotch this time."

ELECTION INTELLIGENCE.

"Montrose Burghs.—Mr. Morley has accepted the invitation to stand."—The Times.

[Westminster Gazette, November 29, 1895.]

VIII.—"SOUVENIRS."

MR. MORLEY: "Look at my Newcastle chair and clock. Very nice, are they not?"

SIR WILLIAM HARCOURT: "Very. Such a nice safe seat! And does the clock strike the items of the Newcastle Programme? Very thoughtful of them. But just look at my lovely Derby tea-service!"

MR. MORLEY: "How sweet of them! Such a pretty reminder of your Local Veto Bill!"

Mr. John Morley was presented with a carved oak chair and a grandfather's clock by his Newcastle friends—lately his constituents—and Sir William Harcourt received a consolation prize from Derby in the shape of a tea-service of the best crown Derby ware.

Westminster Gazette, December [illegible]

IX.—THE EXPULSION OF MR. HEALY.

"OLD PARTY. Oh! do go away, naughty wasp! I can't stand it any longer!"

There had been [illegible] for some time between [illegible] and "Tim" Healy, and at last [illegible] could stand it no longer, and [illegible] away.

[WESTMINSTER GAZETTE, November 29, 189[illegible]

X.—THE NEW IRISH LEADER.

MR. DILLON IN THE SADDLE: "WOA! STEADY!"

Mr. Sexton having definitely declined to accept the leadership of the Irish Party, Mr. Dillon has been elected to the chairmanship by 38 votes to 21, and we can only hope that his tenure of office will be more peaceful than most people are inclined to prophesy is likely to be the case. We trust the statement is true that some of those who voted against him have assured him of their loyal support now that he is actually chosen leader. As for the suggestion that Mr. Healy will endeavour to "cut out" Mr. Dillon in the Parliamentary proceedings, we can only say that Mr. Healy can, if he will, find plenty of scope for his extraordinary ability, without in any way making the running against his leader. In any case, it is much to be desired that we shall have no more differences fought out publicly. If Irish politicians must differ, let them be content to be English to the extent of allowing the fighting to be done behind the scenes.

XI.—THE REAL "SAGES OF CHELSEA."

"He is called almost habitually by a name from which I dissent—the 'Sage' of Chelsea. I think that a sage is just what he was not. In my judgment this is the very last word that ought to be applied to him. I believe I know at least one, and I am not sure that I do not know two, residents of Chelsea at this moment to whom I would more willingly give the name 'Sage' than to Carlyle."—MR. JOHN MORLEY's speech at the Carlyle Centenary, December 4.
[Mr. Leonard Courtney resides in Chelsea—so does Mr. Morley.]

XII.—GREAT BRITAIN AND AMERICA.

THE FAT-BOY IN POLITICS.

(With apologies to the other Fat-Boy in "Pickwick.")

President Cleveland: "Missis! Missis!!"

Mrs. Britannia Wardle: "I am sure I have always had a warm affection for you, Cousin Jonathan; I have always given you a hearty welcome when you have visited me; I invest millions of pounds with you; I buy your cotton and your corn; my bluest blood is poured into your democratic veins. Come now, I have tried to treat you nicely, I'm sure."

President Cleveland: "I know you have."

Mrs. Britannia Wardle: "Well, come, what's the meaning of this?"

President Cleveland: "Missis—I wants to make your flesh creep."

[illegible] the Venezuelan boundary difficulty, and President Cleveland's message to the Senate came as a bolt from the blue. [illegible]

Westminster Gazette, December [illegible]

XIII.—THE ORDEAL OF KING PREMPEH.

"What's the charge, Sergeant?"
"Drunk and incapable, Sir."

"How do you know he's drunk?"
"He can't pronounce *British interests*, Sir."

The King is still drunk. It seems that he was in mortal dread as to what would happen to him when he met Sir Francis Scott, and fortified his nerves accordingly in the orthodox Ashantee fashion.—*Central News telegram from Coomassie, January* 22.

The march to Coomassie is over, and the fabulous King Prempeh is a prisoner. But although the campaign was a bloodless one, poor Prince Henry of Battenberg fell an unworthy victim to the unhealthy climate.

[WESTMINSTER GAZETTE, January [illegible], 1896.]

XIV. THE CONCERT OF EUROPE

"You can blay your own music; but you will take ze time from me."

["What the Sultan wants is a little breathing space, and we hope the Powers will give it."—*Tory Papers*, December 15.]

WESTMINSTER GAZETTE, December 16, [illegible]

XV.—ABDUL THE DOUBLE-HEADED.

The recent accounts of continued massacres in Asia, and the revolting details, prove that, while the Sultan promises with his lips to the Powers, he is acting, *pen in hand*, in the provinces for the extermination of the Armenians.—*Standard's* Correspondent at Constantinople, December 6.

The occasion of these massacres was the pressure put upon the Sultan to carry out certain reforms. . . . The object of the massacres was to nullify these reforms and carry out the established policy of the present Sultan by reducing the Christian population in this territory to an insignificant minority without wealth or influence. This object has been attained—

1st. By killing, in cold blood, a certain number of the leading Armenians in every town.

2nd. By looting the shops and houses of all the Armenians in the towns, thus depriving those left alive at once of their property and their means of living.

3rd. By destroying the Christian villages, and thus reducing the agricultural population, as well as that of the towns, to the alternative of death by starvation or of embracing Mohammedanism.

4th. By completing the work of destruction after the massacres by confiscation, imprisonment and death under the forms of Turkish law.—A Constantinople Correspondent in the *Times*.

[Westminster Gazette, December 9, 1895.]

XVI.—"PEACE WITH HONOUR."—REVISED VERSION.

THE PRIMROSE PATH OF DALLIANCE.

(Ghost of EARL OF BEACONSFIELD: "What! still the Eastern Question? I thought we had settled it with Peace and Honour?"

MARQUIS OF SALISBURY: "Exactly so, my Lord! We still have the *Peace*, but the people are getting doubtful about the *Honour*!"

[WESTMINSTER GAZETTE, January 1, [illegible]]

THE SULTAN: I don't care; they may build as many *Dryads* as they like—they can't hurt me.

The Concert of Europe has degenerated into a farce of dumb [illegible]. But at last it looks as if Great Britain were going to [illegible]. The *Dryad* is ordered to proceed up the Dardanelles, but the next day it [illegible]. Little wonder, therefore, that the [illegible] in the British Navy has no [illegible] over the Sultan of Constantinople.

[Westminster Gazette, February [illegible]]

ABDUL THE PLEASED.

[The Sultan has sent a telegram to Lord Salisbury expressing "grateful approval" for his "Nonconformist" speech.]

Lord Salisbury, speaking at the Nonconformist Unionist Banquet on January [illegible], treated the Armenian question in a way which must have made the Sultan [illegible] with joy.

XVIII.—THE MILK OF HUMAN KINDNESS.

ABDUL THE BENEVOLENT.

XIX.—LORD BEACONSFIELD IS DEAD.

The hon. gentleman is not content with discussing the present situation. He must needs carry his mind back to 1878. He said that Lord Beaconsfield's policy has been a failure. Lord Beaconsfield is dead. What is the object of attacking him?—*Mr. Balfour in the House of Commons, Tuesday, February 11th.*

XX.—THE KAFFIR BOOM IN THE CITY.

The opening up of the Gold-fields of the Rand, and the development of improved processes for the extraction of the precious metal, brought about a speculative fever. For some time past the Stock Exchange has been in a wild state of excitement. Prices have gone up by leaps and bounds, and enormous fortunes have been made. And still the bubble grows. The question is—how long will it be before it bursts?

[WESTMINSTER GAZETTE, October 5, 1895.]

XXI.—THE TRANSVAAL CRISIS.

THE DUET.

"If the Boers chose to raise their voices in singing the 68th Psalm I should have joined them heartily."
Mr. Courtney in the House of Commons, February 13.

"The rebellious dwell in a dry land."

Mr. Leonard Courtney was one of those who [illegible] resisted the mistaken policy of the annexation of the Transvaal, which led up to our war with the Boers. There was therefore nothing incongruous in Mr. Courtney's expression of his willingness to join President Kruger in a thanksgiving service.

XXII.—OOM SALISBURY.

"Give these aliens the franchise? Bah! What I say is, don't let them come in at all!" [While Lord Salisbury and the Government are urging President Kruger to give the franchise to the "aliens" in the Transvaal, they are about to introduce a Bill (see Queen's Speech) to prevent other aliens from even landing in this country.]

XXII.—MR. CHAMBERLAIN AND PRESIDENT KRUGER.

AN UNEQUAL GAME

"Who can play against such cards!"

SYMPATHY.

President Kruger has expressed his sympathy with Mr. Chamberlain.—*Daily Telegraph*.

Oom Paul he play'd a little game
  Of cards with "Pushful Joe;"
But though his cards were far too strong,
  His heart was full of woe.

He felt so full of sympathy,
  For the public didn't know
That all the good cards in the pack
  Were Paul's and—not for Joe.

XXIII

A DIFFICULT PIECE OF MUSIC.

THE GOVERNMENT CREW.

AN APPEAL FROM THE BOWS.

"Oh, *do*, please, get out of the way, your Honour! We were getting on so nicely."

(Westminster Gazette, February [illegible])

XXV.—HOW SOME PEOPLE KEEP THE PEACE.

IN LETTERS TO THE PRESS.

[Picture Politics, January, 1896.

XXVI.—NOT TO BE DRAWN.

A SCENE ON BOARD THE "MOOR."

It is reported that many newspaper correspondents joined the *Moor* at Maderia in the hope of interviewing Mr. Rhodes. Mr. Rhodes, however, declined to be interviewed, or to make any statement. DAILY PAPERS.

All efforts to "draw" Mr. Rhodes [illegible] Mr. Rhodes [illegible] newspaper correspondents [illegible] Mr. Rhodes [illegible] the *Moor* [illegible] Mr. Rhodes to England.

[WESTMINSTER GAZETTE, February 4, [illegible].]

XXVII.

"THE NAPOLEON OF AFRICA."

"THE NAPOLEON OF AFRICA." IS IT HIS MOSCOW.

Recent affairs in the Transvaal have cast a shadow over Mr. Cecil Rhodes. Some people think that Krugersdorp will prove to have been his Moscow.

XXVIII.

THE WOOING OF MISS TRANSVAAL

President Kruger said the other day that the Transvaal Republic was like a maiden wooed by many lovers, and on its being suggested that the maiden was definitely betrothed to John Bull, Oom Paul caustically replied that John Bull had treated his *fiancée* so badly that her affection had been alienated. It is doubtful, perhaps, whether Miss Transvaal wants any lovers dangling about her at all, and whether she would not prefer the simple joys of spinsterhood. But if she cannot keep her wooers away, she might say, "How happy could I be with either were t'other dear charmer away." At present, William appears to be the favourite, but John is not easily got rid of.

[WESTMINSTER GAZETTE, April 28, 1896.]

XXIX "SING A SONG"

Sing a song of Jameson,
Troopers all astray,
Five hundred & ... troopers
All in a pie.

When the pie is opened,
The music ... will sing,
Isn't this a dainty dish
To set before the King?

In 1889 the U.S. government opened up the Oklahoma territory, which resulted in the famous "Oklahoma land rush" as thousands of would-be settlers came racing in to look around, resulting in the famous "rush to get the hell back out of Oklahoma."

Dave Barry

Wednesday
AUGUST

XXX.—"MY OLD DUTCH."

MR. CHAMBERLAIN AND PRESIDENT KRUGER.

(With Apologies to Mr. Albert Chevalier.)

Joe is trying to win back the affection of his "Old Dutch," but she turns a cold shoulder to his advances. He is the more anxious to make it up because the dashing young German William has been [illegible] eyes at the [illegible] direction.

Westminster Gazette.

XXXI. BRER RABBIT IN THE BRIER-PATCH.

"Ain't you gwine to come outer dat brier-patch, Brer Rabbit?" sez Brer Fox, sezee. But Brer Rabbit ain't gwine to come out.

THE INVITATION THAT WAS WITHDRAWN.

President Kruger, after keeping Mr. Chamberlain's invitation open for three months, has finally decided not to come to London. First he would and then he wouldn't, then he said his Volksraad wouldn't let him. As if to remove the anxiety, Mr. Chamberlain solemnly announced to the House of Commons that as Mr Kruger declined to come, he hereby withdrew the invitation. In future, we suppose, it will be the rule in good society, when a man declines your invitation to write back by return of post and tell him to consider the invitation withdrawn.

XXXII.—THE BIG BOSS JOE.

At the Cabinet Council "Mr. Chamberlain wore his usual buoyant manner, and had a white butterfly orchid in his button-hole. A member of the Conservative Party remarked as he passed, '*That is our boss now.*'"—*Daily Chronicle*.

"Boss.—An overseer, or something at least a [illegible] in the [illegible] spirit of [illegible] American [illegible]."—*American Dictionary*.

I'm the big Boss Joe from Birmingham, Oh!
And I'm running just now the Government show;
For Balfour and Salisbury take back seats,
And I take the chair when the Cabinet meets.

When I walk along the streets people say,
What business is he going to boss to-day?
Though Tories may grumble, they'll soon get to know,
I'm the big Boss Joe from Birmingham, Oh!

[WESTMINSTER GAZETTE, November 11, 1895.]

XXXIII.—THE POLITICAL TURVEYDROP.

"LESSONS IN COURT DEPORTMENT GIVEN HERE."

"After luncheon an adjournment was made to the Green Drawing Room, where the Bechuana Chiefs were requested to enter their names in the visitors' book. *Then a little instruction was imparted to the Chiefs as to how to conduct themselves on entering the Royal presence, Mr. Chamberlain acting as tutor.* When the necessary proficiency had been attained the visitors were ushered into the Royal presence." *Daily Paper.*

THE REHEARSAL.

TURVEYDROP: "Now, gentlemen, all at once, please. My son Austen will be the Queen. This way. Advance—bow low—on your knees—kiss the hand—rise—bow—retire backwards. That's very good indeed, Khama. *(Aside)* I had no one to show me. No; *(whispers)* had to do it before my glass."

'Westminster Gazette, November [illegible]

XXXIV.—"PUSHFUL JOE."

"The disposition of England to pick up every unclaimed or ill-protected point of vantage and to dispute the jurisdiction of any other country shows a spirit not unmatched by any nation. I suppose Mr. Chamberlain is the present representative of that *pushful* spirit."—CHIEF JUSTICE ALVEY, *Times*, January 21st.

This picture and the next show our pushful, commercial, up-to-date Joe (see p. 95) in two characteristic attitudes. In the first he is acting as traveller to the firm, pushing his rivals right and left, and leaving them behind him with sore toes and bruised shoulders. In the next, he has just dressed the shop, and is pointing with pride to the splendid arrangement of goods to his new orders. Over the door is an [illegible] which declares that he has a [illegible] to the shop-[illegible]. As he stands in the door he is quite sure that none of his rivals can touch him; but his rivals, on the other hand, are rather apt to take offence at his boastful attitude and depreciation.

(WESTMINSTER GAZETTE, January 24, 1896.)

XXXV. THE GREATEST SHOW ON EARTH

UNDER THE PERSONAL MANAGEMENT OF MR JOSEPH PUSHFUL.

XXXVI.—THE NEW STATESMANSHIP.

NEWSPAPER BOY. "They want more 'copy,' please! There's two columns still to fill."

MR. C.: "Confound it. This is the only thing I've got left. I suppose I'd better let them have it."

["It is not possible to feed the public appetite from week to week and day to day and hour to hour, and then suddenly say to the newspapers accustomed to this luxurious fare, 'I am now going to put you on starvation allowance, and tell you no more what I send or what I receive.'"—*Mr. Balfour in defence of Mr. Chamberlain, House of Commons, Friday, February 14.*]

The New Statesmanship and the newly-invented practice of our great imperial publicists, as soon as he becomes Secretary of State, to conduct his diplomacy in public. Throughout the Transvaal crisis by sent a daily bulletin to the newspapers, concerning his great and splendid doings he had done during the day. He did this, however, some say others. This is one comment of the later despatch to President Kruger perhaps should a great stirror of pained sorrow for Our Emperor ... Mr. Chamberlain sent it to the newspapers before, as it turned out, he had submitted the telegram, and, of course, also long before it could come into President Kruger's hands.

XXXVII. JOHN BULL'S TOUR IN THE SOUDAN.

LORD SALISBURY (agent for Cook and Co.): Your camel is quite ready, sir.
JOHN BULL: But how far am I going?
LORD SALISBURY: You had better leave that to us, sir.
JOHN BULL: That's all very well, but I should like to have a programme. Suppose I'm stopped?
LORD SALISBURY: Then you'll have to come back again.

The [illegible] with regard to the Soudan appears to be that the Expedition [illegible] but the extent of the advance will depend [illegible]

Messrs. Cook [illegible] transport arrangements.

[*Westminster Gazette*, March [illegible]]

THE SOUDAN EXPEDITION.

XXXVIII.

John Bull: Are you strong, Fuzzy Wuzzy?
Fuzzy: Yes! Do you want to fight?
J. B.: Oh! no. I only wanted to know.

The "Go as far as you can but retire if you are resisted" policy in the Soudan.

XXXIX.

THE MAHDI ATTACKING COLONEL PASHA.
(WESTMINSTER GAZETTE, March, 1896.)

XL.
"PUSHFULNESS" IN EGYPT.

(LORD SALISBURY AND MR. CHAMBERLAIN).
Mr. Chamberlain backs up Lord Salisbury in his Egyptian policy.

(WESTMINSTER GAZETTE, May 21, 1896.)

XLI.

SIR WILFRID WATERDRINKER EN ROUTE FOR THE SCENE OF OPERATIONS.

Sir Wilfred Lawson said at Huddersfield that he likes the "Go as far as you can but retire if you are resisted" policy so much that he felt he had to enlist for the Soudan expedition.

XLII POINTS FROM THE BUDGET.

CIGARETTE SMOKING BY THE YOUTHFUL POPULATION.

INDIAN TEA DRIVING CHINESE OUT OF THE MARKET.

SUGGESTION FOR COAT OF ARMS FOR MILLIONAIRE WHO HAS AMASSED A FORTUNE BY PICKING UP CIGAR AND CIGARETTE ENDS.

AFTER THE BOOM IN THE KAFFIR CIRCUS.

THE EVER-INCREASING LOAD OF THAT OLD MAN OF THE SEA, THE ADMIRALTY, WHO SITS ON THE SHOULDERS OF EVERY CHANCELLOR OF THE EXCHEQUER.

Sir Michael Hicks Beach, the Chancellor of the Exchequer, made the annual Budget statement on April 16th. It had been a wonderful year for the Exchequer: every item showed an increase. Tobacco had [illegible] probably owing in part to cigarette smoking by the youthful population. [illegible] Champagne has shown the [illegible] effect of the Kaffir Boom. Indian tea has been driving coffee and China tea out of the market.

Westminster Gazette, April 17, 18[illegible]

XCIII.—THAT TERRIBLE CHILD.

BISHOP (in retreat): "Dear me! How terribly indiscreet and premature!"

[illegible]

XLIV.—THE EDUCATION BONFIRE

MARCH 31, 1896.

Sir John Gorst's Education Bill, which was introduced on the last day of March, was found not only, as was generally expected, to endow Voluntary Schools with further gifts of public money, but to upheave the whole system of elementary education in the country.

School Boards are to be restricted or destroyed, the Cowper-Temple clause will be consumed in the flames of denominationalism, and the Act of 1870 will practically disappear.

Whether Sir John Gorst enjoys his rôle of executioner is open to question, but he is very skilled in the art of partially concealing his private opinions.

Westminster Gazette.

XLV.—THE SCRAMBLE FOR THE CHILD.

Scene: The Hall of a Board School. Time: The Hour for the "Separate Religious Instruction."

Chorus of Eager Denominationalists: "My child!"

[*Our Cartoonist here suggests what must be the result if the Education Bill passes in its present form. All denominations will be at scrambling for the child.*]

'Westminster Gazette,' May 13, 1896.

XLVI.—PREPARED TO DEFEND.

I.—BEHIND THE SCENES

CLERK (Mr. Jesse Collings) *to* EMINENT ADVOCATE (Mr. Pushful Chamberlain): "Please, Sir, here's a new brief. Looks rather a stiff one."

EMINENT ADVOCATE: "Oh! it's all right. I can do it. Here, take the other one, and be sure you return it. (*To himself*) All the same, it's a distinct advantage to know the other people's case."

"At the proper time Mr. Chamberlain will be quite prepared to defend the Education Bill."—LETTER TO THE *BAPTIST*, April 16, 1896.

Mr. Chamberlain announced, through the columns of the *Baptist*, before the Education Bill came on for second reading, that he was "prepared to defend" it. Not unnaturally, therefore, we looked forward to a spirited defence of his protégé at his hands, for we have never concealed our admiration for the ease and agility with which the great Special Pleader does his work. Of course, Mr. Chamberlain, in accepting a brief for the defence, put himself in the peculiarly strong position of a barrister who is able to go into court knowing quite well what his opponent's case is, because he was once briefed for the other side.

WESTMINSTER GAZETTE, April 27, 1896.]

XLVII

"AS DESIGNED BY MR. BALFOUR."

Mr. Balfour [illegible] the Irish Party for the purpose of carrying the Agricultural Rating and the Education Bills through [illegible] a [illegible] carrot in the shape of the Irish Land Bill in front of [illegible]

[WESTMINSTER GAZETTE, April [illegible] 1896.]

XLVIII

XLIX.

THE WALRUS AND THE CARPENTER.

It is difficult to know whether the Education Bill, which was introduced by Sir John Gorst, really represents that gentleman's views, but he played with great success the part of the cynical carpenter to Lord Salisbury's Walrus—the Walrus which means, if he can, to finish up the Board School oysters.

[WESTMINSTER GAZETTE, May 6, 1896.]

"I WONDER HOW YOU CAN DO IT."

Mr. Asquith, in his speech on the Second Reading of the Education Bill, referring to Mr. Chamberlain, said: "I marvelled at his career throughout [illegible] [illegible] days I marvelled at the ease with which [illegible] [illegible] on his head or feet."

[WESTMINSTER GAZETTE, May 6, 1896.]

1.—THE EDUCATION CHAMELEON.

"The thin chameleon, fed with air, receives,
The colour of the thing to which he cleaves."

Dryden.

The chameleon has certain peculiarities which have always made it prominent in political symbolism. It possesses strongly developed prehensile powers, and it has the extraordinary faculty of changing its colour in accordance with that of the objects to which it clings, or by which it is surrounded. [illegible] ... Everybody knows how the Republican and of his younger Birmingham days faded into the less aggressive hue of the old Liberal, and how this, in [illegible], after a [illegible] of [illegible], changed into the true blue of the Tory Party.

Westminster Gazette, May 4, 1896.

II.—THE MINISTERIAL BANK-HOLIDAY.

Decentralisation is the order of the day, and if the population of London goes on increasing as it has done and is doing now, we shall have to decentralise our Bank Holidays, for the cabs are not large enough to enable everybody to get out at the same time. Why not have Bank Holidays in sections for the different classes of the community—Ministerial one day, Clerical another, journalists another, and so on? A Ministerial Easter Monday would be very attractive. Lord Salisbury could indulge in camel riding, with George Curzon behind as camel-boy. Mr. Chamberlain might run a South African shooting-gallery, Mr. Goschen could give John Bull some giddy sensations with a swing-boat, Sir John Gorst would naturally preside over a School Board "cocoa-nut shy," Mr. Balfour would run the Parliamentary Procedure Roundabout to amuse Willie Redmond and Tommy Bowles; while Sir Michael Hicks-Beach would take the money at the turnstile. A favoured few outsiders might be admitted, and the Archbishop of Canterbury could be given the opportunity of an aerial flight, amongst other amusements.

(Westminster Gazette, April 7, 1896.)

PICTURE POLITICS

Do these Cartoons Amuse you? If so, you should Subscribe at once to **PICTURE POLITICS**

The Penny Pictorial Monthly, of Political Premier and Shot, for Political Associations, Parliamentary Candidates, Electors, and all Persons interested in the Work and Workers of Politics of To-day. Illustrated by MR. F. C. GOULD.

CARTOONS OF THE CAMPAIGN. By F. C. GOULD.

THIRD EDITION. PRICE ONE SHILLING. By Post 1s. 3d. Also an *Edition de Luxe*, limited in Number.

The Best Book for a Present.

"WHO KILLED COCK ROBIN?"

And OTHER STORIES for CHILDREN YOUNG and OLD.

By F. CARRUTHERS GOULD.

Half Holidays at the Zoo

IN THE EVENING OF HIS DAYS.

Mr. Gladstone in Retirement.

MILLIONS OF SUFFERERS
In all parts of the Globe have tried

HOLLOWAY'S
PILLS AND OINTMENT.

For every form of disease that can affect the body internally and externally; and the universal verdict is that they are the

BEST, SAFEST AND MOST RELIABLE FAMILY MEDICINE.

Manufactured only at 78, New Oxford Street, London; Sold by all Chemists and Medicine Vendors.

THE BEST SPORTING GARMENTS
are to be obtained of
DR. JAEGER'S
Co., Ltd.
PURE WOOL TAILORS.

Health and Comfort are here combined with the highest examples and best traditions of West-End Tailoring.

Pure Wool Throughout, Protecting from Chill.

ONLY TAILORING ADDRESS:
42, Conduit Street,
New Bond Street, London, W.

Telephone: "HIGHMOST," London."

PUBLICATIONS OF GEO. NEWNES, LTD.
ILLUSTRATED BOOKS.

Vol. 1 of the Navy and Army Illustrated.
with its many hundreds of beautifully printed illustrations, with its gilt edges and handsome cover, forms one of the finest gift books ever published. Price 21s. *Just published*.

New Ground in Norway.
The Ringerike, Telemarken, Sætersdalen.
By E. J. GOODMAN, Author of "The Best Tour in Norway." With 56 Illustrations from Original Photographs by PAUL LANGE. Reproduced in the finest style. The above named work, the first book of Travel in South Norway that has appeared for many years, gives a full and interesting account of the District of Ringerike, Telemarken, and Sætersdalen, and places of interest on the Southern Coast. Price 10s. 6d. *Just published*

Round London.
An Album of 184 Pictures from Photographs of the Chief Places of Interest in and around London. Oblong 4to, cloth extra, gilt, 10s. 6d., half-morocco, 21s.

Round the World,
from London Bridge to Charing Cross, via Yokohama and Chicago.
An Album of 184 Pictures from Photographs of the Chief Places of Interest in all Parts of the World. Oblong 4to, cloth extra, gilt leaves, 10s. 6d., half morocco, 21s.

Round the Coast.
An Album of 184 Pictures from Recent Photographs of the Watering Places and Resorts in the United Kingdom. Oblong 4to, cloth extra, gilt leaves, 10s. 6d., half-morocco, 21s.

"We know nothing of anything like the price which can be compared with these for giving to the sedentary traveller such a true glimpse of what the world, or his own sea-shore contains that is interesting and picturesque."—*Press*

The Sportfolio.
An Album of 140 Portraits and Biographies of Heroes and Heroines of Sport and Pastime. 4to, cloth extra, gilt leaves, 6s.

"Contains many portraits and biographies of well known men and women in the world of sport, and admirably.… a right ornament for one's book-shelf."—*Star*

Zig-Zags at the Zoo.
By ARTHUR MORRISON and J. A. SHEPHERD. 236 pp. super royal 8vo., cloth extra, 3s. 6d.

"*Zig Zags at the Zoo* is a necessary volume to all people who are fond of animals and gifted with a sense of humour."—*Sportsman*
"A most delightful book."—*Glasgow Herald*.

"THREE CASTLES"

CIGARETTES.

Mild and Fragrant. Manufactured from the Finest Selected Growths of Virginia.

THE

"THREE CASTLES"

TOBACCO.

MILD AND FINE CUT (Green Label) specially adapted for Cigarettes.
MEDIUM STRENGTH AND COARSE CUT (Yellow Label) strongly recommended for Pipe Smoking.

W. D. & H. O. WILLS, LTD., BRISTOL & LONDON.

PRICE ONE SHILLING.

THE WESTMINSTER CARTOONS

No. 3.

— 1899. —

BY

F. Carruthers Gould

PUBLISHED BY

The Westminster Gazette, Tudor Street, Blackfriars, E.C.

F. CARRUTHERS GOULD, Esq.,

WRITER OF

The SWAN FOUNTAIN PEN

"I find your 'SWAN' PEN excellent for Cartoon work. The nib does not corrode as ordinary steel pens do, and it gives a firm, even line without the scratchiness which is so great a difficulty when drawing in pen and ink with a free hand."

For Longhand, Shorthand, Pen-and-Ink Drawing, Music-writing, indeed, whenever a Pen is necessary, use only a "SWAN."

Made in 3 Sizes at

10/6
16/6
25/-
up to
18 Gns.

Post Free.

Adds immeasurably to Celerity and Comfort in writing.

Of all Pens most famous.

Test one at the earliest opportunity.

EVERY ARTIST SHOULD USE THE "SWAN."

Complete Illustrated Catalogue Post Free on application to

MABIE, TODD & BARD,

93, CHEAPSIDE, E.C., 95a, REGENT STREET, W., LONDON,
And 3, Exchange Street, MANCHESTER.

SELECTED GIFT BOOKS.

PHOTOGRAPHIC ALBUMS.

ROUND THE WORLD. From London Bridge to Charing Cross, via Yokohama and Chicago. 281 Photographic Pictures of the Chief Places of Interest in all parts of the World, with descriptive text. Oblong 4to, cloth extra, gilt leaves, **10s. 6d.**

ROUND THE COAST. An Album of 281 Pictures from recent Photographs of the Watering Places and Resorts in the United Kingdom, with descriptive text. Oblong 4to, cloth extra, gilt leaves, **10s. 6d.**

ROUND LONDON. An Album of 281 Pictures from Photographs of the Chief Places of Interest in and around London, with descriptive text. Oblong 4to, cloth extra, gilt leaves, **10s. 6d.**

THE THAMES ILLUSTRATED. A Picturesque journeying from Richmond to Oxford. 161 large and 170 small Photographic Plates, with descriptive text. 4to, cloth extra, gilt leaves, **10s. 6d.**

ALL ABOUT ANIMALS. 250 Illustrations of Animal Life, from Photographs by Gambier Bolton, F.Z.S., and others, with explanatory text. Oblong 4to, cloth extra, gilt leaves, **10s. 6d.**

ENGLAND'S HISTORY, as Pictured by Famous Painters. An Album of 256 Historical Pictures, with descriptive text. Edited by A. G. Temple, F.S.A. Oblong 4to, cloth extra, gilt leaves, **10s. 6d.**

REFERENCE BOOKS.

THE CITIZEN'S ATLAS. Comprising 160 Maps and Gazetteer. Edited by J. G. Bartholomew, F.R.G.S. Crown folio, cloth extra, **16s.** net; half-morocco, **18s. 6d.** net.

THE ORACLE ENCYCLOPÆDIA. Profusely Illustrated. Edited by R. W. Egerton Eastwick, B.A. (of the Middle Temple). Complete in 5 vols., price **30s.**

"The most Extraordinary Pennyworths which even this age of Cheap Books has seen."

Post Free, 2d. each.

TIT-BITS MONSTER ALMANACK, 1898. 80 pages One Penny. Facts and Figures for Everyone.

TIT-BITS MONSTER FAIRY BOOK. 80 pages. One Penny. Veritable Tit-Bits for the Little Folks. Old favourite Fairy Tales retold.

TIT-BITS MONSTER RECITATION BOOK. 80 pages One Penny. Simple, Pathetic, Humorous, and Patriotic Poems suitable for Recitation, with Hints on Elocution.

TIT-BITS MONSTER COOKERY BOOK. 80 pages One Penny. Palatable and Economical Dishes for Breakfast, Dinner, Tea, and Supper. No foreign phrases or fanciful concoctions.

TIT-BITS MONSTER TABLE BOOK. 80 pages. One Penny. British, Foreign, and Colonial Weights, Measures and Money Tables, Tables of Distance, the Metric System.

GEORGE NEWNES, LIMITED,

Southampton Street, Strand, London.

THE

WESTMINSTER CARTOONS

Vol. III.

A PICTORIAL HISTORY OF POLITICAL EVENTS

FROM

1896–1898

BY

F. CARRUTHERS GOULD.

London:

THE "WESTMINSTER GAZETTE" TUDOR STREET, E.C.

1899.

PREFACE

The Cartoons and Drawings in this Volume appeared in the "Westminster Gazette," the "Westminster Budget," and "Picture Politics."

Although not arranged in strict chronological sequence, they cover all matters of political interest from November 1896 to November 1898.

The Cartoons deal with a variety of subjects. The earlier ones, after touching on the Motor-Car movement which set in towards the end of 1896, refer to the incidents of the Jameson Raid and the subsequent proceedings of the South Africa Committee with its inconclusive result.

Mr. Chamberlain's influence on the Tory Party is depicted in connection with the Workmen's Compensation Bill.

Next comes the Jubilee, showing Mr. Chamberlain's "abundant performance" with the Colonial Premiers in his train, and some suggestions of things that were omitted from the Jubilee Procession.

The policy of France towards this country is foreshadowed by a Cartoon of M. Hanotaux making hay whilst the Salisbury sun shines. Then follow illustrations of the appointment of Mr. Darling to the Judicial Bench, and the Religious Difficulty in the London School Board contest.

In 1898 the year opens with a Cartoon dealing with the Report of the Old Age Pensions Committee. The London County Council Election comes next, concluding with the hurried drowning of the Government's Municipal Government Cat. Then Lord Salisbury goes away, and at Easter time Ministers are cheered with the acquisition of Wei-hai-Wei.

At the end of May the passing of Mr. Gladstone is typified.

Then we see Mr. Chamberlain as Joeydicea on the war-path, and again as trying to induce President Kruger to say "Suzerain."

Next he figures with his "Long Spoon" speech. China then comes to the front in various aspects, Sir William Harcourt and the Ritualist controversy follow, and we are brought to recent events connected with the Soudan expedition and the Fashoda question. Finally, we have the German Emperor in Palestine, and an attempt to illustrate the Poet Laureate's "Pax Britannica."

CONTENTS.

TOPICAL CARS FOR TOPICAL PEOPLE.

I.—The Archbishop of Canterbury's Auto-Motor.

TOPICAL CARS FOR TOPICAL PEOPLE.

II.—The British Foreign Office [illegible] "Hard Labour" Private Motor Car.

Westminster Gazette, December 4, 1906.]

III.—THE JAMESON RAID.

From the Bayeux Tapestry up-to-date.

No. 1. JAMESON, with others, raideth across the borders of the Transvaal. He encountereth the Boers, is overcome, and surrendereth.

No. 2. KRUGER casteth his captives into gaol. Joseph is perplexed. Rhodes cometh to Joseph, but departeth quickly.

No. 3. KRUGER releaseth the captives, who are carried by ship to England. They are haled before the Magistrate, who committeth them for trial. They are tried by three Judges, and are condemned to imprisonment for a time.

[Westminster Budget,
Christmas Number, December 11, 1896.

IV.—SHADOWS OF THE SOUTH AFRICA COMMITTEE.

Mr. Labouchere.

Sir Rd. Webster.

Mr. Jackson.

V.—SHADOWS OF THE SOUTH AFRICA COMMITTEE.

VI.—THE GRAVE OF THE SOUTH AFRICA COMMITTEE.

A MONUMENT OF FAILURE.

Chief Mourners—Mr. Jackson and Sir Rd. Webster.

[Westminster Gazette, June 11, 1897.]

VII.—THE END OF THE GAME.

Chorus of South Africa Committee (all except Mr. Blake and Mr. Labouchere.)—"Well, if we can't safely do anything else, we can all sit on Rhodes. That won't hurt anyone."

[Westminster Gazette, July 15, 1897.]

VIII.—TURNING THE OLD PARTY UPSIDE DOWN.

PROFESSOR CHAMBERLAIN teaches the Old Party how to stand on his head.

(Look at this picture upside down, and it will be seen that the title of the party operated on has not been changed.)

Mr. Chamberlain, in his speech on Tuesday week on the Workmen's Accidents Bill, proved completely, to his own satisfaction—that the Tories are the real Liberals, and that Mr. Bright and Mr. Cobden were the real Tories.

[WESTMINSTER GAZETTE, May [illegible].]

IX.—THE APT PUPIL

"On the last occasion I had to hold the Old Party's legs, but you will observe, gentlemen, that he is now able to stand on his head without the slightest assistance."

[Westminster Gazette, July [illegible].]

X.—LADY LONDONDERRY'S PROTEST.

LADY LONDONDERRY: "Really, my Lord, I'm surprised at you—a man of your age and position!"

We have shown in previous Cartoons how Lord Salisbury, under the tuition of Mr. Chamberlain, has mastered the trick of standing on his head and performing acrobatic feats with the Workmen's Compensation Bill. [illegible] and she has, in the *Nineteenth Century*, administered a severe rebuke both to pupil and master.

[WESTMINSTER GAZETTE, September 3, 1897.]

XI.—AN ABUNDANT PERFORMANCE

"Her Majesty's Government could only take refuge behind the abundant performances of their distinguished colleagues."—LORD SALISBURY at Trinity House.

XII.—THINGS OMITTED FROM THE JUBILEE PROCESSION.

No. 1. Mr. Speaker.

No. 2. The House of Commons.

Mr. Bartley — Ashmead-Bartlett Pasha. — The First Lord of the Admiralty. — The Home Secretary.

No. 3. The Music of the South Africa Committee.

[Westminster Gazette, June 1897.]

XIII.—MAKING HAY WHILST THE SUN SHINES.

Encouraged by Lord Salisbury's "graceful concessions" in the matter of Tunis, and urged on to fresh triumphs by the French Colonial Party, M. Hanotaux is turning his attention to securing a "settlement" of outstanding questions between Great Britain and France in West Africa.

[Westminster Gazette, October 5, 1897.]

XIV.—FROM ONE SAFE SEAT TO ANOTHER.

LORD H———Y.—"Sit up there, my little DARLING. You'll be in good company, for I put all the others there myself.

Mr. Darling, M.P., is made a Judge.

[WESTMINSTER GAZETTE, October [illegible], 1897.]

XV.—THE RELIGIOUS DIFFICULTY

Little Board School Boy: "Please, where do I come in?"

XVI.—POLITICAL ORDERS OF ARCHITECTURE.

No. 1. Corinthian.—"The florid Corinthian exuberance of Sir William Harcourt."—Lord Dufferin at Leith.

[Westminster Gazette, December 7, 1897.]

No. 2. Ionic.—"The staid Ionic chastity of Mr. John Morley."—Lord Dufferin.

[December 8, 1897.]

No. 3.—Ego and Tongue Moulding (Composite Order).—Omitted by Lord Dufferin.

[December 11, 1897.]

XVII.—THE REV. JOHN BULL & Co.

Some National Missionaries.

Mr. Jesse Collings, speaking at Barnstaple last week, said: "Some of them believed in Missionaries. Did they not also believe in Missionary Nations?"

[Westminster Gazette, December 17, 189[illegible].]

XVIII.- THE CUPBOARD WHICH WAS BARE.

The Old Age Pensions Commission in their Report did not recommend any specific plan. The consequence is that the Commission has had no positive result whatever.

Old Mother Hubbard went to the cupboard *
To fetch her poor dog a bone †
But when she got there, the cupboard was bare, ‡
And so the poor dog had none §

* The Aged Poor Pensions Com[illegible] † [illegible] Aged Poor. ‡ Nothing specific. § Just what he might have expected.

XIX.—THE BEAR AND THE BEEHIVE.

"Why couldn't you leave it alone? You're always blundering into mischief!"

Lord Salisbury made a speech on the Municipal Government of London which did excellent service for the Progressives during the then pending London County Council Election.

[WESTMINSTER GAZETTE, November 30, 189[illegible].]

XX.—THE CAT IN THE BAG.

(It is announced that the London Government Bill will not be produced until after the London County Council Elections.)

MR. CHAMBERLAIN: "Do, for heaven's sake, ARTHUR, keep it in. If that cat is let out of it's bag before the Election, we are done for."

Mem. for Electors who don't want that cat let loose.—Vote for Progressives.

[WESTMINSTER GAZETTE, February 18, 189[illegible].]

XXI.—"DING DONG BELL—PUSSY'S IN THE WELL."

AFTER THE LONDON COUNTY COUNCIL ELECTION

"Get him out of sight as quick as you can, Austen; somebody will be sure to be asking where he is."

XXII.—WELL OUT OF IT.

LORD SALISBURY (who is just starting for abroad): "Good-bye, boys! I wish you joy of it."

[WESTMINSTER GAZETTE March [illegible]]

XXIII.—HI-TIDDLEY-HI-TI-WEI-HAI-WEI!

Ministers start for their Easter holidays.

[Westminster Gazette, April 6, 1898.]

XXIV.—ON THE WEARY WAY-HIGH-WAY.

The Easter Holidays being over, Ministers, having spent all their money, come back to work.

(In the meantime, the proper pronunciation of our new acquisition in China is declared to be Way-high-way.)

XXV.—IN MEMORIAM.

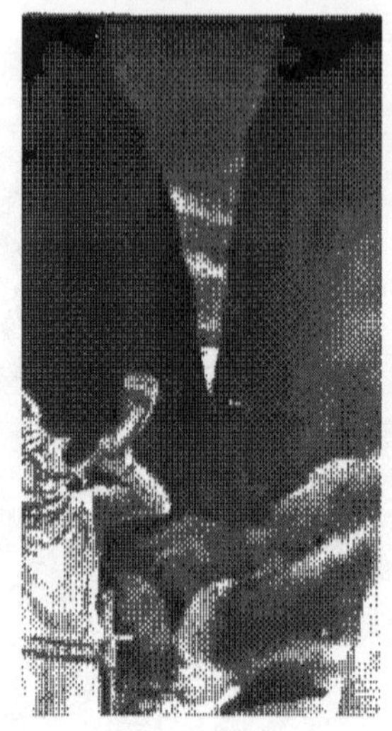

XXVI.—JOEYDICEA ON THE WAR-PATH.

This statuary group, which it is suggested should be erected at Westminster, is in plaster.

N.B.—There are no reins to the horses.

[Westminster Gazette, May 18, [illegible]]

XXVII.—"SAY 'SUZERAIN'!"

"Confound you! Say 'Suzerain'!"

(But up to now the bird will only say "Convention.")

(*Westminster Gazette*, May 31, 1898.)

XXVIII.—AN EGYPTIAN FRAGMENT.—I.

Jo—seph and the Long Spoon.

An interesting feature in the above fragment, which has recently been discovered, is that it proves the adage, "One needs a long spoon to eat with the Devil," to be extremely ancient in its origin. Chaucer has it:—

"Therefore behoveth him a ful long spone that shall ete with a fende."

But this Egyptian tablet shows that the saying was known ages even before Chaucer. The seated figure represents Jo—seph, who was evidently a person of note during the dynasty of the Pharaohs, probably a Court Chamberlain. He is sitting with a flower in one hand, and holding a long spoon in the other. Above him is a cartouche, with a single eye surrounded by a circle. Behind him is a hieroglyphic inscription, showing a lion rising from a crown, or ornamental scroll, and other devices. This inscription has been translated by an Egyptologist, "I hold firm," or, "I run the show."

The second figure represents the Devil surmounted by a double-headed bird. This, probably, refers to some northern Power, at that time threatening the land. The discovery of this tablet is, therefore, doubly interesting, both from the historical and from the literary point of view.

[Westminster Gazette, June 6, 1896.]

XXIX.—EGYPTIAN FRAGMENTS—II.

Another interesting discovery has been made. Golf, as we know, is an ancient and Royal game, but the fragment pictured above shows that it was played in the time of the Pharaoh. The two figures are represented in the act of driving from the tee, and apparently the clubs of the period differed very little from the present type. From the hieroglyphic inscription we gather that the two Egyptian golfers were brothers, and that both occupied important positions in the Court. They were Secretaries of State, probably [illegible], for one of the provinces of Egypt. This is denoted by the barge, the trefoils, and the Secretary Birds which figure amongst the signs. The [illegible] on the tall stalks in front of the leading figure are probably some personal allusion, as is also the battering-ram which appears under the Secretary Bird on one side of the tablet. The three pots and the sacred Ibis indicate that one of the Brothers was a writer on questions of religious philosophy.

XXX.—SOUR GRAPES

"Oh! Mr. Bear, what a mistake you're making in eating those grapes! They'll give you such pain! I'm so sorry for you!"

"I think Russia has made a great mistake in taking Port Arthur."—Lord Salisbury at the Albert Hall, May 4.

[Westminster Gazette, May 6, 1898.]

XXXI.—THAT TERRIBLE CHINA.

"Worse than fifty days of Joseph
Is a railroad in Cathay."—TENNYSON (adapted).

"[illegible]
[illegible]
[illegible]
That flow through gloomy chasms!"

Lord Salisbury, speaking to a deputation from the Associated Chambers of Commerce on Wednesday, said:—"All the rivers flow at right angles to the proposed line, and through chasms of great depth, and there are ranges which would alarm a very experienced

XXXII.—AN UNQUIET RUBBER

"I have often thought that an English Minister, contesting with foreign Powers, is very much in the position of a player at whist who has got a very noisy and talkative friend behind him, who insists on discussing, in the hearing of all present, the value of the various cards in his hands. Meanwhile, the two adversaries, in absolute silence, absolutely destitute of all inquisitive friends, pursue their plans in silence."—Lord Salisbury at the United Club dinner, June 24, 1898.

It will be noticed that Lord Salisbury, having no ally, is playing dummy.

[Westminster Gazette, July 4, 1898.]

XXXIII.—NOT A BOWER OF BLISS.

XXXIV.—A THEOLOGICAL CONTROVERSY.

Sir W. H.: "You be disestablished!"
Rev. [illegible]: "Oh! what shocking profanity"

[Westminster Gazette, June [illegible]

XXXV.—LONG SPOON AND LONG BILL.

A New Version of an Old Fable.

Mr. G**ch*n : "My Bill's as long as your Spoon."
Mr. Ch**b*rl**n : "Yes, and now we can go and have supper with the Bear."

[Westminster Gazette, July 25, 1898.]

XXXVI.—FEELING HIS WAY.

"What's Round the Corner?"

[Westminster Gazette, September 14, 1898.

XXXVII.—AN EGYPTIAN FRAGMENT.

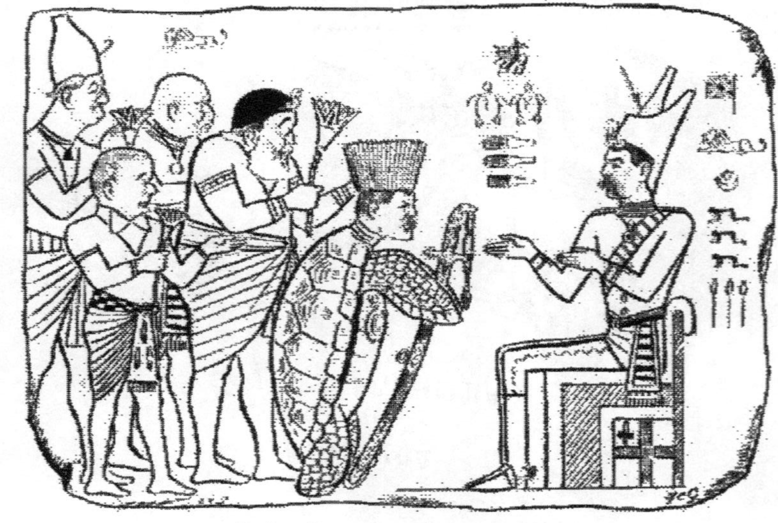

The Lord Mayor presents a Sword to the Sirdar.

[Westminster Gazette, November 4, [illegible].]

XXXVIII.—TEACHER, LEADER, AND EDUCATOR.

MR. CHAMBERLAIN: *I, too, have to educate our Party.*

"The fact is that since the time of Lord Liverpool the position of the Conservative Party has greatly changed, and has changed with great rapidity during the past ten or twenty years. . . . And who was their teacher? Who was their leader? It was Mr. Disraeli who laid the seeds of this doctrine in his great novel of 'Sybil.' Though he found his Party slow to educate, yet they made such progress under his guidance, and under the subsequent guidance of Lord Randolph Churchill and others, that they have now arrived at a position when they may fairly claim that it is to their efforts and to their legislation that the great social reforms now impressed upon the Statute-book of this country are due."—MR. CHAMBERLAIN at Manchester, 17th November, 1898.

WHICH IS TOD SLOAN?

Tod Sloan, we need hardly say, is an American jockey who has introduced a novel method of riding, and the fact that he has won several races has created some excitement in sporting circles. In the above cartoon our artist suggests that Lord Rosebery's method of riding the British Lion comes nearest to the new idea. Sir Michael Hicks-Beach rides hard, but uses whip and spur too much; whilst Lord Salisbury bumps along in the old diplomatic style. We leave it to our sporting readers to decide for themselves which is the style best calculated to win.

[WESTMINSTER GAZETTE, October 27, 1898.]

XL.—MAKING UP FOR LOST TIME.

"I MUST HURRY UP WITH MY LION. I'M A LITTLE LATE."

[WESTMINSTER GAZETTE, [illegible] 17, 1898.]

XLI.—LITTLE BILLEE IN PALESTINE

(With apologies to Thackeray and the Kaiser.)

"I see Jerusalem and Madagascar,
And North and South Amerikee,
And the Prussian fleet a-lying at anchor
With Admiral Wilhelm of Germanee."

Do these Cartoons Amuse you? If so, you should Subscribe at once to

PICTURE POLITICS

The Penny Pictorial Monthly, of Political Powder and Shot, for Political Associations, Parliamentary Candidates, Electors, and all Persons interested in the Work and Warfare of Politics of To-day. *Illustrated by* MR. F. C. GOULD.

[illegible]

[illegible]

UNIFORM WITH "WESTMINSTER CARTOONS," No. 3.

CARTOONS OF THE CAMPAIGN. By F. C. GOULD.

THIRD EDITION. PRICE ONE SHILLING. By Post, 1/3. Also an *Edition de Luxe*, limited in Number.

[illegible]

THE WESTMINSTER CARTOONS (No. 2).

THE STORY OF THE 1893 SESSION, By F. C. GOULD. POPULAR EDITION, ONE SHILLING. Also an *Edition de Luxe*.

[illegible]

Now Ready. Crown 8vo, 144 pages, price 1s., by post 1s. 3d.

ARCHIE, or THE CONFESSIONS OF AN OLD BURGLAR.

By CHARLES MORLEY.

[illegible]

The Best Book for a Present.

[illegible]

NOW READY. [illegible]

"WHO KILLED COCK ROBIN?"

And OTHER STORIES for CHILDREN YOUNG and OLD.

Told in Pen and Pencil.

By F. CARRUTHERS GOULD.

LIBRARY EDITION. [illegible]

THE DOLLY DIALOGUES.

By ANTHONY HOPE, Author of "The Prisoner of Zenda," [illegible]

[illegible]

NOW READY. [illegible]

IN THE EVENING OF HIS DAYS.

BEING A STUDY OF

Mr. Gladstone in Retirement.

[illegible]

[illegible] TUDOR STREET, WHITEFRIARS, LONDON, E.C.

ADVERTISEMENTS.

EVEN THE MOST
EMINENT MEN
DISAGREE ON
SOME POINTS, BUT
EVERYONE AGREES THAT

HOLLOWAY'S
PILLS AND OINTMENT
ARE THE
BEST HOUSEHOLD MEDICINES.

They have held front rank for upwards of Sixty years.

HOTEL CECIL AND RESTAURANT.

Overlooking the Victoria Gardens and Embankment.

Bedrooms from 6s. per day, including Light and Attendance.

LUNCHEONS, DINNERS, AND SUPPERS.

ORCHESTRA DAILY.

"CAPSTAN"

NAVY CUT TOBACCO

Can now be obtained in Three Grades of Strength, viz.:

"MILD." Yellow Label.

"MEDIUM." Blue Label.

"FULL." Chocolate Label.

In 1-oz. Boxes, and in 2-oz., ¼-lb., and ½-lb. Patent Air-Tight Tins.

W. D. and H. O. WILLS, Limited, BRISTOL and LONDON.

THE WESTMINSTER CARTOONS.

VOL. IV.

A Pictorial History of Political Events connected with South Africa, 1899-1900.

BY

F. CARRUTHERS GOULD.

London:
"The Westminster Gazette," Tudor Street, E.C.

1900.

PREFACE.

The Cartoons and Sketches in this Volume have been selected from those which have appeared in the "Westminster Gazette," the "Westminster Budget," and "Picture Politics," and they deal with the different events of the day bearing upon the difficulty between this country and the South African Republics.

The volume gives what is practically a Pictorial History of the negotiations which ended with the outbreak of hostilities and of the political situations created at home by the course of the War.

The first Cartoon suggests the altered attitude of the German Emperor towards the Transvaal, as shown by the interest which he took in Mr. Cecil Rhodes during his visit to Berlin in March, 1899.

Then follows the struggle between the Colonial Minister and President Kruger over the negotiations about the Franchise and other questions affecting the Uitlanders.

President Kruger is shown sticking to his position as the Caterpillar that won't be blown down, and after a time Mr. Chamberlain appears as Sim Tappertit grinding up his tools and hoping that "human gore" may not result.

The Cartoon depicting Mr. Chamberlain as Bellona dragging John Bull into war, although not in accordance with the Colonial Minister's recent declaration that all through the negotiations he clung to peace, proves to have been a correct forecast of the drift of things. The negotiations went on between Brer Fox and Brer Rabbit, and the latter played his seven years' franchise card.

Then came the "Hour-Glass" speech, and Sir Alfred Milner and Mr. Chamberlain are shown giving the Rabbit a last squeeze.

A humorous incident intervenes. Mr. Cecil Rhodes sent a lion to Mr. Kruger, but he would have none of it. In the beginning of October war comes on the scene, and the grim skeleton Scout on the Veldt, with his bodyguard of vultures, is a presage of the inevitable casualties to come.

The war fever runs high, and King "Joe" for the moment rides as proudly as did King John at Her Majesty's Theatre.

The Boer shows fight, and a month later we see Mr. Bull beginning to get critical over his disappointments, and to ask his Ministers for explanations. Parliament met in October to ask for money, and Mr. Chamberlain's Highbury speech and his conduct of the negotiations came under discussion. The German Emperor came to this country in November on a visit to the Queen, and Mr. Chamberlain went to Windsor to see him, great curiosity arising from this as to what game they were after. In his speech at Leicester Mr. Chamberlain trod heavily on French corns, and his attempt to pose as Mr. Turveydrop teaching deportment roused a storm of anger on the other side of the Channel. But M. Blowitz came to his rescue in a message crowded with a delightful mixture of metaphors.

An incidental effect of the war is shown in a cartoon in which Mr. Chaplin tells an Aged Workman not to mention Old-Age Pensions—but to talk about the War.

The successive reverses met with by our troops in South Africa had by this time roused strong feeling in the country. Was it pushfulness or parsimony, or the two combined, which had put us in so humiliating a position?

Some of the Ministerial journals thereupon started scapegoat hunting, and Mr. Balfour, who had defended himself at Manchester on the philosophic plea of the Inevitable was subjected to a heavy bombardment. The surprise exhibited by Mr. Balfour and Sir Matthew White Ridley at the discovery that the Boers had both horses and rifles is also depicted.

The problem on the Tugela River, where the Lion could not get on and the Tortoise would not come out, was still unsolved when the Parliamentary Session of 1900 opened. Ministers resolved, however, as Sir Matthew White Ridley put it, to face Parliament with a cool head, although the shrinkage in their reputation must have been painfully evident to themselves as regards each other. Lord Salisbury took the line that it was impossible to see through the obscure, but Mr. Chamberlain adopted a bolder line. "The curse of the Raid hangs round you still," said Sir William Harcourt in his speech during the debate on the Address. But Mr. Chamberlain's attitude was one of contemptuous indifference, and the last but one of the Cartoons in this Volume illustrates that attitude. The Government had a large majority on the division which followed the attack on them, for John Bull means his horses to cross the stream, and has no idea of "swopping" in the middle.

The smaller Sketches also deal with aspects and incidents either directly or indirectly connected with the War.

CONTENTS.

I.—"MY FRIEND THE KAISER."

Mr. Cecil Rhodes: My friend the Kaiser.
Oom Paul: Your friend! I thought he was *mine*.

(Westminster Gazette, March 16, 1899.)

II.—THE CATERPILLAR THAT WON'T.

The Farmers in one of the Eastern States of America have found out that if they blow horns and trumpets under their fruit trees the Caterpillars tumble to the ground, and can be destroyed with ease. Mr. Chamberlain wishes he could do the same with the Oom Caterpillar, which declines to tumble.

[Westminster Gazette, June 14, 1899.]

III.—THE WRESTLERS.

In this interesting Toy the figures wrestle violently, but they do not get any "forrader."

[WESTMINSTER GAZETTE, June 16, 1893.]

IV.—A FELLOW FEELING.

OLD SALISBURY (to OOM PAUL): Cheer up, old chap; I can sympathise with you; I've been through it all myself. It's very horrid to extend the franchise, but we've got to do it sometimes and make the best of it.

[WESTMINSTER GAZETTE, June 20, 1898.]

V.—A HEATED SPIRIT.

"I'll grind up all the tools. Grinding will suit my present humour well. Joe!"

Whirr-r-r.

The grindstone was soon in motion; the sparks were flying off in showers. This was the occupation for his heated spirit.

Whirr-r-r-r-r-r.

"Something will come of this!" said Mr. Tappertit, pausing as if in triumph, and wiping his heated face upon his sleeve. "Something will come of this. I hope it mayn't be human gore!"

—"Barnaby Rudge," ch. IV.

[Westminster Gazette, July 6, [illegible].]

VI.—THE "STATESMAN'S GAME."

"War is the Statesman's Game."

John Bull (to Bellona): War? Where—why—when? What's it going to cost, and what good will come out of it?

[Westminster Gazette, July 11, [illegible].]

AT LAST!

Bravo! Buller!

"It's dogged as does it."

(Westminster Gazette, March 1, 1900.)

"WHO SAID 'BOBS'?"

THE TORTOISE LOOKS OUT.

[WESTMINSTER GAZETTE, February [illegible], [illegible].]

VII.—THE POINT.

"W'at sorter seasonin' d'you sagashuate I'se gwineter cook you with, Brer Rabbit?" sez Brer Fox, sezee Brer Rabbit up en say he don' warrer he cooked 't all.

Brer Fox he grit his teef. "Youer gittin' 'way from de point, Brer Rabbit," sez Brer Fox, sezee.

[Westminster Gazette, July 14, [illegible].]

VIII.—WAITING FOR THE RED GLOW.

An adaptation from "Barnaby Rudge."

[Westminster Gazette, July 13, 1895.]

IX.—BRER RABBIT PLAYS A CARD

Brer Coon (peeping in at the door): Spec I'll better cut inter dis game sum time erwhiles.

[Westminster Gazette, July 20, 189[illegible].]

X.—THE HOUR-GLASS AND THE EIGHT-DAY CLOCK.

"We were told the other day that the sands in the hour-glass were running down. I would not have an hour-glass yet. I would have the good, steady, old-fashioned eight-day clock. If they have not got one at the Colonial Office there is one at the Foreign Office."—Mr. John Morley, at Arbroath, September 6, 1899.

[Westminster Gazette, September 7, 1899.]

XI.—SQUEALING AND SQUEEZING.

Mr. Chamberlain and Sir Alfred Milner: Why do you keep on squealing "Suzerainty"?

Boer Rabbit: I can't help squealing, you squeeze me so hard!

[Westminster Gazette, September 9, 1899.]

XII.—IN THE COLONIAL WARD.

Nurse Chamberlain: Here's your draught, Mr. Kruger.

Mr. Kruger: Is there any horrid uncertainty in it?

Nurse Chamberlain: No, there isn't; so you'd better drink it up quickly and get it over.

[But Mr. Kruger wouldn't.]

[Westminster Gazette, September 14, 1899.]

XIII.—THE NASTY LION.

(With Apologies to [illegible].)

—Take the lion away,
O take the nasty lion away,
I won't have any lion to-day.—

(N.B.—The lion's mane has been "cropped.")

Mr. Cecil Rhodes has presented President Kruger with a lion for the Pretoria Zoo.

[Westminster Gazette, September 19, [illegible].]

XIV.—THE SCOUT ON THE VELDT

[Westminster Gazette, October 4, [illegible].]

XV.—HER MAJESTY'S KING JOE.

On His War Horse.

(Suggested by a sketch in the *Daily Chronicle* of "King John" at Her Majesty's Theatre.)

[Westminster Gazette, September [illegible], 1899.]

XVI.—WHY NOT?

It is reported that President Kruger is anxious to go to the front and fight. On the principle of "Let those who make the quarrels be the only ones to fight," why should not Mr. Chamberlain also take the field himself?

(Westminster Gazette, October 18, 1899.)

XVII.—SHOWING FIGHT

The Wild Boar and the Shadow of the Lion

[Westminster Gazette, October [illegible], [illegible].]

XVIII.—WHICH IS THE REAL KRUGER?

THE THEORETICAL KRUGER.
(Measured by Lord Salisbury.)
"An amiable and sensitive old man."

THE GENERAL WEYLER OF THE TRANSVAAL.
(Suggested by Mr. Chamberlain's letter to the London correspondent of a New York journal, in which he compared Transvaal to Cuba.)

THE GOOD OLD PAUL.
An ideal figure cherished by many

[WESTMINSTER GAZETTE, October 19, 1899.]

XIX.—THE NEWEST DIPLOMACY.

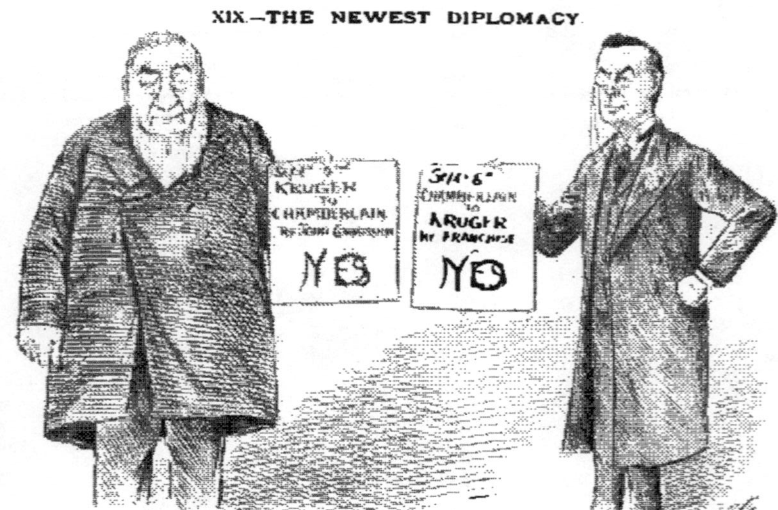

NEGATIVE-AFFIRMATIVE OR AFFIRMATIVE-NEGATIVE.

CHAMBERLAIN (to Kruger): Do you accept my proposal about the Joint Commission?

KRUGER: No—yes.

KRUGER (to Chamberlain): Do you accept my proposal about the franchise?

CHAMBERLAIN: Ye—no.

[SEQUEL. As they fail to understand each other they get to fighting.]

[WESTMINSTER GAZETTE, October [illegible], 1899.]

XX.—MR. CHAMBERLAIN'S GOLD CASKET.

The above is a suggested design for the gold casket which it is proposed to present to Mr. Chamberlain at the Guildhall.

[Westminster Gazette, October [illegible]]

XXI.—POT AND KETTLE.

THE AMENITIES OF THE CABINET KITCHEN.

"I remember, for instance, a speech, which was very much applauded by right hon. and hon. gentlemen opposite of my noble friend the Prime Minister at a Guildhall Banquet."—Mr. CHAMBERLAIN, in the House of Commons, October 25, 1899.

[WESTMINSTER GAZETTE, October 27, 1899.]

XXII.—MR. BULL BEGINS TO BE CRITICAL

Mr. Bull: You should have had more men out there before you bluffed.
Mr. Chamberlain: Oh, but we couldn't, sir; those dreadful Radicals——
Mr. Bull: Don't tell me that—with your majority of 160—the fact is, you bluffed before you got your cards.

[Westminster Gazette, November 2, 1899.]

XXIII.—A MUTUAL PLEASURE.

The London correspondent of the *Western Daily Mercury* stated that the Kaiser had expressed a desire to meet Mr Chamberlain during his visit to England.

Said the Kaiser to Joe,
"You're praised, I know,
So I very much wanted to meet you."

Said Joe to the Kaiser,
"I own that I try, Sir,
But it's hopeless to think I can beat you."

[Westminster Gazette, November 16, 1899.]

XXIV.—THE POINTER AND THE MAN BEHIND THE GUN.

WHAT GAME ARE THEY AFTER?

(Suggested by Mr. Chamberlain's visit to the German Emperor at Windsor.)

XXV.—MR. TURVEYDROP'S ACADEMY.

Mr. Turveydrop, having finished his German pupil, turns his attention to Miss France.
"We do our best to polish - polish—polish!"

Mr. Turveydrop in "Bleak House."

[Westminster Gazette, December 4, [illegible].]

XXVI.—MIXED METAPHORS.

M. de Blowitz (with the blood of Don Quixote gliding through the veins of Sancho Panza): Do not kick the fallen Lion!

["Really this unanimity of hostile criticism can be compared only to the attacks which a few weeks ago assailed the charming actress of the Théâtre Français, Mlle. Lara, when she took the part of Froufrou. ... Yet when I behold this universal outcry, when I see everyone falling upon this speech; above all, when I see, now that he is thought well down, all the besotted individuals following him up to give the lion a kick—the lion, I repeat, of the day—I feel a little of the blood of Don Quixote glide through the veins of Sancho Panza, and I am tempted to step forward as the champion of this speech."—M. de Blowitz on Mr. Chamberlain, in the Times, December 8, 1899.]

[Westminster Gazette, December 9, 1899.]

XXVII.—REJECTED ADDRESSES.

FRANCE: You are horrid—and I hate you.

AMERICA: Guess you're going a bit too far.

GERMANY: You presume too much.

(WESTMINSTER GAZETTE, December 8, [illegible].)

XXVIII.—"DON'T MENTION IT!"

Mr. Chaplin (to Aged Workman): "Old Age Pensions! 'Sh—don't mention it—let's talk about the War."

["I have often been under obligation to my hon. friend, but I do not know that I ever felt more indebted to him than when he told you just now he had abandoned all intention of asking me to-night to express my view, and the opinions and intentions of her Majesty's Government, with regard to the very vexed question of Old Age Pensions. I accept with gratitude the invitation of your chairman to confine my observations to that question which occupies the mind of everybody at the present moment, namely, the progress of the war in South Africa which has been forced upon us."—Mr. Chaplin at the United Club dinner, December 9, 1899.]

[Westminster Gazette, December 15, 1899.]

XXIX. PUSHFULNESS AND PARSIMONY.

SIR MICHAEL to JOE: It's all the fault of your beastly pushfulness!

JOE to SIR MICHAEL: It's all the fault of your beastly parsimony!

JOHN BULL: You're both right, and a pretty mess you've made of it between you. Now, then, you can clear out, I'm going to take this job in hand myself.

[Mr. Chamberlain's visit to Ireland is a courageous act, but its political wisdom at this juncture is gravely questioned. The speech at the Leicester luncheon, in the opinion of some of the right hon. gentleman's most ardent supporters, renders a [illegible] of his country than himself. I am able to state that it is the belief of some of the Opposition leaders that [illegible] in the field render the retirement of Mr. Chamberlain from the Ministry a matter of certainty.

[WESTMINSTER GAZETTE, December 18, 1899.]

"The refusal of the Chancellor of the Exchequer to provide the funds for preparations declared to be necessary by the military authorities will presumably involve the retirement of Sir Michael Hicks-Beach from the Cabinet."—Observer, Sunday, Dec. 17, 1899.]

XXX. THE GARDEN THAT HE LOVES.

Dr. Tyrrell, in introducing Mr. Chamberlain at Dublin, referred to his love of orchids in a Latin sentence which we venture to translate, "Let us rather praise those flowers of oratory with which he, the happy gardener, is wont to sway and delight every mob and every club."

[Westminster Gazette, December 21, 189[illegible].]

XXXI.-THE SCAPEGOAT-HERD

Driving the Scapegoats out into the Wilderness.

N.B.—The one in the background is hoping that he has been overlooked.

[Westminster Gazette, January 6, 1900.]

XXXII. THE TUGELA PROBLEM.

THE LION: Come out!

THE OOM TORTOISE: Come on!

[WESTMINSTER GAZETTE, January [illegible], [illegible].]

XXXIII.—THE ABSENT-MINDED ONE.

"What a horrid noise! I wonder whom they are firing at?"

[WESTMINSTER GAZETTE, January 16, 1900.]

XXXIV. SUCH A SURPRISE.

MR. BALFOUR: Fancy, Ridley! they've actually got horses!

SIR M. W. RIDLEY: And look, Arthur, they've got rifles too! What a shame to deceive us!

[Westminster Gazette, January [illegible]]

XXXV. GETTING THEIR HEADS COOL.

"It might be that her Majesty's Ministers were to a certain extent on their trial, but they would face Parliament with a cool head."—Sir MATTHEW WHITE RIDLEY, at Blackpool, January 18, 1900.

(Westminster Gazette, January [illegible], 1900.

XXXVI.—SHRINKAGE.

(With apologies to Bovril.)

[Westminster Gazette, January [illegible].]

XXXVII.—THE OBSCURE AND THE OBVIOUS.

LORD R.: What's the matter?
LORD S.: I can't see through this wall.

LORD R.: Why not get a ladder?
LORD S.: I can't afford it—they won't let me have any money.

(WESTMINSTER GAZETTE, February 8, 1898.)

XXXVIII. THE ANCIENT MARINER.

["The curse of the Raid hangs round you still."—Sir W. Harcourt, in the House of Commons, February 8, 1900.]

The Ancient (and Wily) Mariner: Let it hang! *I* don't mind.

[Westminster Gazette, February 7, 1900.]

XXXIX. NO "SWOPPING"

John Bull: No, I'm not going to swop them now. They'll have to get through this job first.

In writing on the result of the York Election we referred to the sentiments of the "man in the street," and said: "He is seriously troubled at the apparent lack of knowledge, foresight, and judgment displayed by her Majesty's advisers. But, to use his familiar phrase, he is not prepared to swop horses in crossing the stream, and the deeper the holes into which they plunge the more determined he is to keep them at it. So he whips his Ministers and votes for them at the same time, postponing his judgment of them until the other bank is reached."

[Westminster Gazette, February 9, 1900.]

XI.—PEOPLE WHO THOUGHT IT WOULD BE SO EASY.

I.—The Music Hall Jingo.

[Westminster Gazette, December 15, 1899.]

II.—The [illegible] Patriot.

"Buy 'em, my vriend, buy 'em till you're black in the face. Vy, it'll be all over in a veek ven we get out there."

[Westminster Gazette, December 21, 1899.]

III.—General Blazer at the Rag.

"Rubbish, sir! Give me a Division and I'd guarantee to be in Pretoria in a fortnight."

[Westminster Gazette, December 27, 1899.]

XLI. VOLUNTEERS WHO *MIGHT* GO TO THE FRONT.

I.—Mr. Arthur [illegible]

[Westminster Gazette, [illegible] 1899.]

II.—Rev. Hugh Price Hughes.

[Westminster Gazette, October 16, 1899.]

III.—Mr. Dillon Going to the Front.
(Suggested by Mr. Johnston of Ballykilbeg.)

[Westminster Gazette, October [illegible] 1899.]

IV.—Mr. W. Redmond, Mr. Swift MacNeill, and Mr. P. O'Brien on a [illegible] Raid.

[Westminster Gazette, October [illegible], 1899.]

I.—THE INVISIBLE INEVITABLE.

"How on earth am I to know what's inside? I can't see through a stone wall!"

["I would ask, how were we to know? I believe, as a matter of fact, though this must not be taken as official, that the guns were generally introduced in the boilers of locomotives, and that the ammunition was truly introduced in piano cases and tubs. No doubt President Kruger, who is a shrewd man, succeeded in accumulating great armaments without, until very recently, arousing any suspicion of their enormous size. But the noble lord seems to think that that is an elementary matter which we were bound to know. You cannot see through a stone wall."—LORD LANSDOWNE in the House of Lords, January 30, 1900.]

[WESTMINSTER GAZETTE, February 1, 1900.]

II.—AN ABSENT-MINDED ONE.

"The man in the street knows as much as the man in the Cabinet."—MR. BALFOUR, at Manchester, January 8, 1900.

[WESTMINSTER GAZETTE, January 10, 1900.]

III.—THE INEVITABLENESS OF THE ABSENT-MINDED.

["I do not know a single war which has begun triumphantly for this country."—MR. BALFOUR at Manchester, January 9, 1900.]

MR. BULL: You seem to have got the worst of it. What's the matter with your arm?

THE ARMY, ABSENT-MINDED ONE: Oh, only the hand of Fate and inevitable incidents.

[WESTMINSTER GAZETTE, January 11, 1900.]

IV.

"L'ADDITION."

Who sups with Mr Chamberlain must expect a long bill.

[WESTMINSTER GAZETTE, February 14, 1900.]

XLIII.

I.—THE MINSTREL YEOMANRY TRUMPETER.

[He thought that, perhaps, our [illegible] might [illegible] corps of Yeomanry, each of the poets mounted on his own Pegasus, provided with an adequate [illegible] of words, and to [illegible] the [illegible]. With regard to the [illegible] and [illegible], they might [illegible] —Mr. Alfred Austin at the Authors' Club, January 22, 1900.]

[Westminster Gazette, January [illegible].]

II.—THE "CHAMBERLAIN" ARTILLERY EQUIPMENT.

A. The [illegible] Sponge. C. Long Table-spoon.
B. [illegible] D. "Joe Chamberlain" Gun.
E. Details of Long Table-spoon.

[Contracts have been placed in Sheffield and Birmingham for 170,000 table-spoons for the Army.]

[Westminster Gazette, January 4, [illegible].]

III.—A VERY LITTLE ENGLAND VIEW.

[The *Daily Mail* recently published a portrait of the German Emperor with the inscription, "A friend in need is a friend indeed."]

"A Friend in Need is a Friend Indeed."

The (*Daily Mail*) Lion: It's *so* good and kind of you to come just now; I'm in such trouble.

Kaiser: My dear Leo, I've only come over *just* for a few days' shooting.

[Westminster Gazette, November [illegible].]

IV.

The Bill that Grew.

[Westminster Gazette, February [illegible].]

WESTMINSTER CARTOONS. No. 5.

Price One Shilling.

THE KHAKI CAMPAIGN.

GENERAL ELECTION, 1900.

By F. CARRUTHERS GOULD.

Deutz & Geldermann,

"Gold Lack"

EXTRA QUALITY

Champagne.

Deutz & Geldermann "Gold Lack" Champagne can be obtained of all Wine Merchants, and at Leading Hotels and Restaurants.

BEST VALUE ON MARKET.

Roper Frères et Cie.,

1st Quality *Champagne.*

VINTAGE 1892. VINTAGE 1893.

ROPER FRÈRES 1st Quality extra dry.
ROPER FRÈRES 1st Quality medium dry.

THE

KHAKI CAMPAIGN.

WESTMINSTER CARTOONS.

GENERAL ELECTION, 1900.

BY

F. CARRUTHERS GOULD.

PREFACE.

At no previous General Election have political cartoons been used so freely, both as leaflets and posters, as during the one just concluded.

The fact that both sides have made so large a use of pictorial attacks, arguments, and appeals, shows that the picture has come to have a practical value in political warfare.

We make no apology, therefore, for publishing in a collected form the cartoons and sketches which appeared in the "Westminster Gazette," the "Westminster Budget," and "Picture Politics," immediately before and during the General Election of 1900.

Some of them, particularly the one entitled "Political Slimness," were reproduced in colours and issued as Liberal Posters. Although intended to influence the public mind, we venture to think that they are none of them offensive to our political opponents or out of harmony with the ethics of fair fighting.

The "Quarterly Review" in its October number expresses the opinion that our caricaturist "F. C. G." was a little too savage towards the end of the electoral struggle, but as in the same article Mr. Chamberlain is severely rebuked for the methods which he adopted in dealing with his opponents, "F. C. G." may reasonably excuse himself by pleading that it was the "dog" and not the caricaturist that grew savage.

The first six cartoons in the collection deal with the looming of the General Election on the political horizon. According to popular rumour there was a strong desire on the part of some of the members of the Cabinet to dissolve Parliament and appeal to the country in the Autumn, a desire which was supposed to be resisted by others who disliked, as Lord Beaconsfield disliked, to snatch a party advantage out of a national occasion, or, to use Lord Beaconsfield's own words, "to dissolve merely with the object of gaining an advantage at the polls due to transitory circumstances." But whatever truth there may have been in these rumours, the "pushful" party had their way, the Khaki pot was set boiling, and the Dissolution took place. The one issue, it was declared, was the war. All other questions were to be subordinated, and as for inquiries into such details as the conduct of the war, Mr. Brodrick said "Hush!" Everything would be inquired into when the Election was over. From the Liberal point of view this appeared like sheltering behind the victorious figure of Lord Roberts, and the point is illustrated by the cartoon "Political Slimness," in which Lord Salisbury, Mr. Balfour, Mr. Chamberlain, Lord Lansdowne, Mr. Goschen, and Sir Matthew White Ridley are represented taking advantage of "cover." The same point is accentuated in the picture of Lord Salisbury afloat with Mr. Chamberlain in a Khaki hat, whilst another represents all the Ministers in the dressing-room getting into the popular uniform before going on the stage.

On the other side we see Lord Rosebery hurrying down the steps of the slip to get into the Liberal boat before it sails out to face the storm. Several of the following cartoons deal with Mr. Chamberlain's Election speeches and his method of winning votes by imputing, to put it mildly, a lack of patriotism to his opponents. But after the "dog" had ramped round biting people, Mr. Balfour appears as the consoler with a timely display of graceful manners.

How the Mayor of Mafeking's words, which played so large a part in speeches and posters on the Unionist side, became crystallised is exhibited in a drawing of some historical tapestry discovered at Bradford.

After the election was over, further political slimness is shown in the retirement of Ministers to the hills carrying the votes which they had looted from the electorate.

Another cartoon illustrates the peculiar fact that whilst the General Election here has been fought in Khaki by the Government, in the American Presidential Election Mr. McKinley is just as anxious to get rid of his Khaki coat as Mr. Chamberlain was to put his on.

Amongst the remaining cartoons three—"The cupboard was bare," "Lo the poor Indian," and "Such a surprise"—are reproduced again, as they figured largely amongst the literature with which the Liberals fought their battle.

CONTENTS.

I.—THE BOILING POINT.

WORKING THE CHARM.

"Dissolution, toil, and trouble:
Fire, burn; and, cauldron, bubble."

"MACBETH" (revised).

"—— In regard to the question of popularity, it is submitted that, even if the present enthusiasm should cool down somewhat in the interim, it will inevitably reach boiling point again when the troops begin to return from the front."
—*The Times* on the Prospects of a Dissolution, May 29, 1900.

[WESTMINSTER GAZETTE, May 30, 1900.]

II. PASTING THEM OVER.

BILL-STICKER: What a relief to get rid of all this common electioneering stuff.

("I have every confidence in an appeal to [illegible] (the [illegible]); but I have [illegible], if the record of the Unionist Party be behind us and only common local electioneering is before the people."—Letter from a Conservative Member to the Times, May [illegible], [illegible].)

(Westminster Gazette, May [illegible], [illegible].)

III.—A QUESTION OF DISSOLUTION.

WILL THEY DISSOLVE?

[*Westminster Gazette*, July 27, 1900.]

IV.—"HUSH!"

MR. BRODRICK (to John Bull): Hus-sh! Not a word! Wait till the election is over, and then we'll inquire into everything.

[Westminster Gazette, September 8, 1900.]

V.—ON THE BRINK.

Mr. C. (to Lord S.): Come, take 'em off and jump in. The longer you wait the colder it will get.

(Westminster Gazette, September 7, [illegible].)

VI.—THE BLUNDER-FOX AND THE RED HERRINGS.

A Fable.

Once upon a time a Blunder-Fox was much troubled in his mind how he should elude his pursuers. Noticing his distress, two kind-hearted Red Herrings went to him and said: "Have no fear. When the hounds approach we will cross your path, and that enable you to escape your foes."

During the General Election campaign Majuba and Khaki were the favourite "red herrings" used by Tory candidates to throw voters off the scent of the Government's blunders.

[Westminster Gazette, September 11, 1900.]

VII.—POLITICAL SLIMNESS

A Khaki Issue.

Lord S.: Get under cover—don't expose yourselves!

[Westminster Gazette, September 18, 1900.]

VIII.—"IMPOSSIBLE!"

MR. BULL: Want to stay on! But you've made such a mess of everything!
MAJOR DOMO: Well, sir, there may have been some inevitable mistakes, but we might have done much worse.
MR. BULL (*emphatically*): IMPOSSIBLE!

[WESTMINSTER GAZETTE, September 19, 1900.]

IX.—ON A KHAKI SEA.

"The Tory Party's gone afloat,
[illegible] where it has no [illegible];

It's all of us in a Khaki boat,
Upon a Khaki Ocean."

MR. C.: Isn't this jolly?
LORD S.: H'm—I'm a little too old for this sort of thing.

[WESTMINSTER GAZETTE, September [illegible], [illegible].]

X DRESSING UP

Ministers in the Dressing Room preparing to go on the Stage

[Westminster Gazette, September [illegible], 1900.]

XI.—SKETCH NOTES OF A SATURDAY NIGHT'S STUMP SPEECH

BY A POLITICAL CHEVALIER.

No. 1.

"If you wouldn't buy my 'taturs in this street—d'ye think I'd take 'em into the next street an' offer 'em to a lot o' bloomin' furriners? Not for joe! I'd burn the barrer an' I'd drown myself fust."

["If they were ever to turn against him—forgive the supposition—his political career would come to an end. He had been so proud to represent his fellow citizens that he could not stoop to ask the suffrages of any other constituency. He would not seek a refuge amongst other [illegible]."—MR. CHAMBERLAIN in West Birmingham on Saturday, September 22.]

No. 2.

"I wish all you coves in this street 'ad plenty of money in yer pockets—cos why? Cos then yer'd all buy my 'taturs."

["He wished in his heart they had Manhood Suffrage in that Division. He was sure it would only increase the number of his friends."—MR. CHAMBERLAIN in West Birmingham on Saturday, September 22.]

No. 3.

"Don't you believe what those chaps on the other barrers say. They tell sich lies! Why, there's two 'undred an' twenty thousand sojers of the Queen—they're all awye in Afriky. They've all got wotes, every man Jack of 'em, and they'd all buy my 'taturs if they was 'ome."

["If they had considered party interests alone, would the Government have taken the election now, when there were 200,000 men—soldiers of the Queen—all of whom were voters—away in South Africa?"—MR. CHAMBERLAIN in West Birmingham on Saturday, September 22.]

[WESTMINSTER GAZETTE, September 28, 1900.]

XII.—MANNING THE BOAT.

LORD R.: Hold hard a moment! I'm coming aboard.

(WESTMINSTER GAZETTE, September [illegible], [illegible].)

XIII.—NO CHANGES.—(1.)

It is stated that beyond the resignation of Mr. Goschen there will be no changes in the Ministry should the Unionists return to Office after the General Election.—Daily Paper.

Lord Salisbury will continue to watch over the interests of the Empire in all parts of the world.

The Duke of Devonshire will continue to look after the important interests of Education and will keep the reformers "in their proper places."

[Westminster Gazette, September 26, 1900.]

XIV.—NO CHANGES (II.)

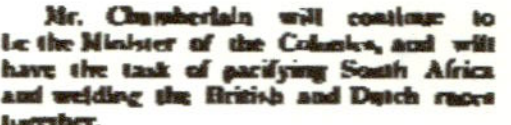

Mr. Chamberlain will continue to be the Minister of the Colonies, and will have the task of pacifying South Africa and welding the British and Dutch races together.

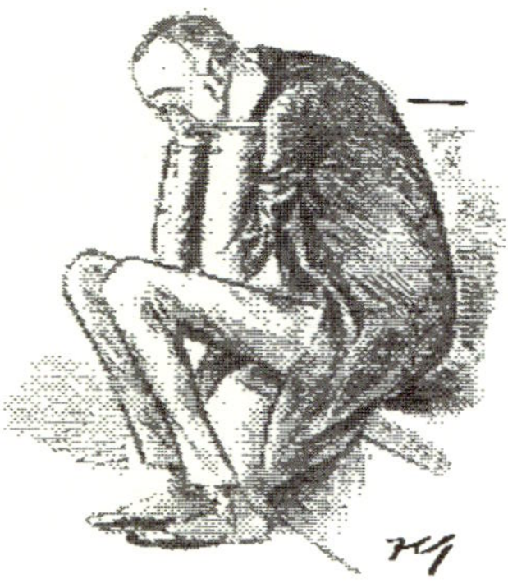

Mr. Balfour will continue to have charge of the business of the country in the House of Commons, and, "being a child" in such matters, he will continue to "know no more than the man in the street"—except about golf and bimetallism.

XV.—NO CHANGES.—(III.)

Lord Lansdowne will continue to manage the War Office.

He will be supported by Mr. Powell Williams, of Birmingham, who will continue to look after minor details, such as Boots, Helmets, Horses, and Guns.

[Westminster Gazette, September 29, 1900.]

"Look at me and my friend the Dook. We was 'orrible sinners once, our wickedness was downright 'orful. Why, we acshully 'elped ter give back the Transvaal to them depraved Boers, and after Majuba too! Think o' that, now. So I sez, 'Friends all, if you comes across any ones like wot me and him was, don't vote for 'em. Cast 'em out and call 'em traitors. My friend the Dook 'll tell yer the same w'en 'e wakes up.'"

(Westminster Gazette, September 28, 1900.)

I.—I WAS SO YOUNG.

Mr. Chamberlain tried to get over the difficulty of the fact that he, as well as the Duke of Devonshire, was a member of the Cabinet in the Government which gave back the Transvaal to the Boers after Majuba by saying "I had only just joined the Cabinet." This suggestion that Mr. Chamberlain was so modest and retiring and so abashed by his new honour that he sat with his finger in his mouth and said nothing, like the good little boy who must be seen and not heard, is too imaginative for us to accept. We have tried, however, to realise it in black and white.

[Westminster Gazette, September 28, 1903.]

II.—THAT "BLESSED" WORD.

"I will now go back to what we were talking about—old-age pensions. I do not like that ... of that word."—Mr. Chamberlain in the Carlton Theatre, Birmingham, Saturday, September 19.

[Westminster Gazette, October 8, 1903.]

XVIII.—HIDING THE CORPSE

Ministers had to try and hide the naked corpse of the Government record under the Union Jack.

[Westminster Gazette, October 1, [illegible].]

XIX.—THE KHAKI KIT.

"I dare say I look very well in khaki, but this kit is beastly heavy and uncomfortable."

[WESTMINSTER GAZETTE, October 8, 1900.]

XX.—"WHERE DO I COME IN?"

LORD S. (reading Mr. Chamberlain's speeches): H'm! he says a lot about the Colonial Secretary, but where does the Prime Minister come in?

[WESTMINSTER GAZETTE, October 3, 190[illegible].]

XXI.—METHODS AND RESULT.

UNCLE: I am afraid, Arthur, that he has obtained it by methods which do not quite accord with our—h'm—traditional dignity. But although we would not do such a thing ourselves we are not responsible, of course, for what Joey does when he is off the chain.

NEPHEW: Exactly so, Uncle; I do not myself like the—h'm—methods he has adopted—but it would be Quixotic to refuse to benefit by the result.

[WESTMINSTER GAZETTE, October 4, 1903.]

XXII.—THAT DOG AGAIN.

LORD S. (hastily closing door): Good gracious! I hope he won't try to get in here.

The Tory Party is beginning to be anxious as to what the dog will turn his attention to when he has done killing Liberals.

[WESTMINSTER GAZETTE, October [illegible], [illegible].]

XXIII.—CHRISTIAN CONSOLATION.

Mr. Balfour (to a defeated Liberal): My dear sir, of course you're an "honourable and patriotic" man; and as for those placards, how could I have supposed that they would have been taken literally?

[See Mr. Balfour's speech at Pudsey on October 8.]

[Westminster Gazette, October 11, 1900.]

XXIV.—FROM BIRMINGHAM TO BINGLEY.

A Timely Display of Graceful Manners.

"We are quite genteel now!"

["Three days later, speaking at Bingley, Mr. Balfour was under the painful necessity of explaining that such words as his colleague had used were not to be taken as meaning that every man who voted for a Radical desired the victory of the Boer cause."—*Quarterly Review*, October, 1900.]

[Westminster Gazette, October 18, 1900.]

XXV.

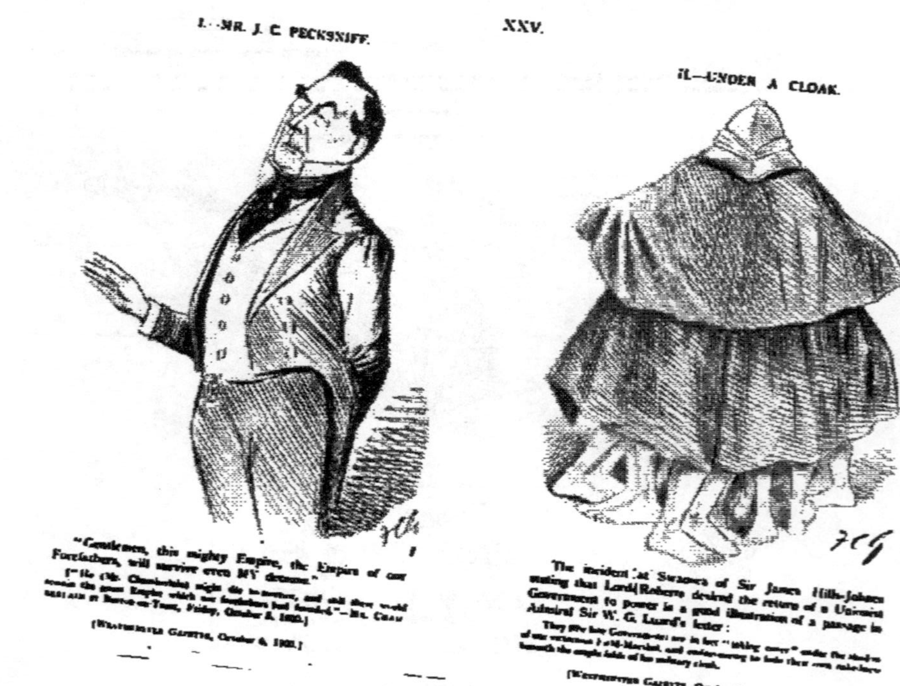

I.—MR. J. C. PECKSNIFF.

"Gentlemen, this mighty Empire, the Empire of our Forefathers, will survive even MY demise."

["He (Mr. Chamberlain) might die to-morrow, and still there would remain the great Empire which our forefathers had founded."—Mr. Chamberlain at Burton-on-Trent, Friday, October 5, 1900.]

[Westminster Gazette, October 6, 1900.]

II.—UNDER A CLOAK.

The incident at Swansea of Sir James Hills-Johnes stating that Lord Roberts desired the return of a Unionist Government to power is a good illustration of a passage in Admiral Sir W. G. Luard's letter:

They (the late Government) are in fact "taking cover" under the shadow of our victorious Field-Marshal, and endeavouring to hide their own nakedness beneath the ample folds of his military cloak.

[Westminster Gazette, October 3, 1900.]

XXVI.—THE FROG AND THE BULL.

THE FROG TO THE BULL:
Roll on, John Bull, roll on
'Cross trackless land and sea,
Roll on!
What tho' I cease to be?

What tho' one day by fate accurst
'Cute Master Joe comes off the worst?
What tho' my puffed-up skin may burst?
Never YOU mind!
Roll on!

(WITH APOLOGIES TO MR. W. S. GILBERT.)

["There was that immortal sentence in his recent speech at Burton-on-Trent, 'I might die to-morrow and still there would remain the great Empire.' It was worth having a General Election to arrive at that truth. If that speech had not been made, the people might never have known that the British Empire would survive Mr. Chamberlain. This was really the intoxication of a man after a debauch of vanity. They knew the fable of the frog who swelled itself out to imitate the ox, and said, 'When I burst the ox will still remain.'"—SIR WILLIAM HARCOURT in West Monmouthshire, October 10, 1900.]

(WESTMINSTER GAZETTE, October 12, 1900.)

XXVII.—A BOGY SCORE

Mr. C.: Ha! I wonder what I'd have done without you!

[Westminster Gazette, October 6, 1903.]

XXVIII.—A CONVERSATION.

(Unauthorised Version, but Highly Probable.)

Sir W. Laurier: "Are you there? Have you done on your side?"

Mr. Chamberlain: "Very nearly."

Sir W. Laurier: "I'm just beginning over here. Can you give me any tips?"

Mr. Chamberlain: "Only one—give 'em Khaki. It's good business. Call them traitors."

Sir W. Laurier: "What's the use? Tupper's about as Khaki as they make them."

Mr. Chamberlain: "That's awkward. Well, call him a Liberal Imperialist and say he's a traitor."

Sir W. Laurier: "But I happen to be a Liberal Imperialist myself, and Tupper isn't a Liberal, and he isn't a traitor."

Mr. Chamberlain: "You're extraordinarily squeamish on your side. What's good enough for us is good enough for you."

Sir W. Laurier: "Oh, no, it isn't, and I'm not going to do it. Besides, haven't you said yourself that we're all enthusiastic Imperialists?"

Mr. Chamberlain (irrelevantly): "Well, then, Tupper 'll call you a traitor. Somebody's got to do it to somebody. It's no use having a Khaki election unless somebody does it. Have you got any letters?"

Sir W. Laurier: "I don't understand."

Mr. Chamberlain (impatiently): "What's the sense of having a Khaki election, if you haven't got any letters? Didn't Tupper write to Kruger?"

Sir W. Laurier: "Most improbable."

Mr. Chamberlain: "Do you mean to tell me you never had the mail-bags searched?"

Sir W. Laurier (indignantly): "Of course I didn't."

Mr. Chamberlain: "Then what's the use of coming to me? You're starting a Khaki election, and you haven't any letters, and you won't call anyone a traitor. You'd better come to Birmingham and take a lesson before next time. I think I'll call up Sir Charles Tupper."

Sir W. Laurier: "He's running your Zollverein."

Mr. Chamberlain: "Ha! Most decidedly I'll call up Tupper."

[Westminster Gazette, October 16, 1900.]

XXIX.—CRYSTALLISATION.

From an old Historical Tapestry recently discovered at Bradford.

[Mr. Wanklyn, M.P., has divulged the process of evolution by which the opinions of the Mayor of Mafeking were "crystallised" (the word is Mr. Wanklyn's) for political use, and we have also learnt how they were recrystallised by Mr. Chamberlain for service at the General Election.]

[Westminster Gazette, October 16, 1900.]

I.—HIS DEPARTMENTAL MANNER

Mr. Powell Williams, now that the election is over, has resumed his official manner.

("I have only to add that this is my final word upon the matter, as it is impossible for me, now that the election is over, to carry on a controversy in the Press upon a Departmental matter."—Mr. Powell Williams in a letter to the Times, October 17.)

[Westminster Gazette, October [illegible], 1900.]

II.—THE MAD DOG AND THE MAN

"The man recovered from the bite."

[Notwithstanding the prejudice created by Mr. Chamberlain's publishing Mr. John Ellis's letter as if it were a part of a treasonable correspondence, Mr. Ellis was re-elected for the Rushcliffe Division of Notts.]

[Westminster Gazette, October 18, 1900.]

XXXI.—"EVERY CONFIDENCE, BUT ——"

OLD TORY PARTY: Very glad to see you back, my lord, which I did my best for [illegible] every confidence in you. The war was be-eutiful! But don't you think, my lord, you might find the gentleman who managed it something else to do?

[It is a little singular that the Tory Party, having expressed their confidence in the Government in response to an appeal on the [illegible] of the war, there'd be an [illegible] to suggest that if Lord Lansdowne "wishes to retire from the War Office" some other post might be found for him—say, the Lord Lieutenancy of Ireland.]

[WESTMINSTER GAZETTE, October [illegible].]

XXXII.—MORE SLIMNESS.

After the Raid.

Ministers having suddenly swooped upon the constituencies and looted the Electorate retire to the hills, where they are safe from attack, and will probably not be seen again during the next three months.

[Parliament will not assemble until the end of January or the early part of February.]

[Westminster Gazette, October 22, 1900.]

XXXIII.—THE DECORATIONS AND THE BILL

"H'm—rather crude and extremely loud, don't you think so, Arthur? Has he sent in his bill yet?"

"Not yet, sir; but I'm afraid it will be pretty stiff."

(Westminster Gazette, October 23, 1900.)

XXXIV.—KHAKI—HERE AND THERE

Mr. Chamberlain: Why, Mr. President, what are you getting out of your khaki in such a hurry for?

President McKinley: You'd do the same if you were in my place. I should lose my election if I were seen in it.

Mr. C.: That's funny—I won mine with khaki.

President McK.: Yes—but they've had more time to think about it over here.

Lord S.: I'd like to get out of mine—it's beastly uncomfortable, and it doesn't suit me a bit.

(Westminster Gazette, October 20, 1900.)

XXXV.—"THE CUPBOARD WAS BARE."

The Old-Age Pensions Commission, in their report, recommended no specific plan. The result was that the Commission had no positive result whatever.

Old Mother Hubbard went to the cupboard*
To fetch her poor dog a bone†
But when she got there the cupboard was bare‡
And so the poor dog had none.§

* The Aged Poor Pensions Commission. † Pensions for Aged Persons. ‡ Nothing specific. § Just what he might have expected.

[This Cartoon, together with the three following ones, was largely used by the Liberals as posters and leaflets during the General Election contests.]

[Westminster Gazette, January, 1895.]

XXXVI.—"LO THE POOR INDIAN."

MR. BALFOUR: Give you a dole! Quite impossible, my poor fellow. I feel very much for you, but I have heavy family claims.

[WESTMINSTER GAZETTE, July 30, 1903.]

XXXVII.—SUCH A SURPRISE.

MR. BALFOUR: Fancy, Ridley! they've actually got horses!

SIR M. W. RIDLEY: And look, Arthur, they've got rifles too! What a shame to deceive us!

[WESTMINSTER GAZETTE, January 2[illegible], 1900.]

XXXVIII.—PART OF THE PANTOMIME.

"Won't Joey be pleased!"

[Westminster Gazette, May [illegible]]

XXXIX.—THE STRAIN OF STRENGTH.

"Legislation indeed! Why, it's trouble enough to keep up our strength without doing anything."

["I have noticed that, whenever compliments are paid to us by our friends the Opposition upon our great Parliamentary strength, they always seem to be made with the object of inducing us to do something or other that would inevitably result in a diminution of that strength."—The Duke of Devonshire, at the Liberal Union Club Dinner, May [illegible], 18[illegible].]

[Westminster Gazette, May [illegible], 18[illegible].]

XL.—MORE MONEY WANTED.

A MIDSUMMER NIGHT'S DREAM OF THE FUTURE.

Mr. Bull finds it easy enough to borrow, but the worry will come when he has to pay—pay—pay.

[The Chancellor of the Exchequer [illegible] on July [illegible] that he proposed to borrow [illegible] millions more.]

[WESTMINSTER GAZETTE, July [illegible], [illegible].]

XLI.—THE CAT, THE KITTEN, AND THE ARCHBISHOP.

THE ARCHBISHOP (indignantly): Why—it's your own Kitten!

But although the Cat killed the Kitten, Care does not seem likely to kill the Cat.

[illegible]

[illegible]

XLII.—THE INFANT JOSEPH.

"But Joseph was too young to begin French, though he was familiar with 'The Guide to Knowledge,' 'Little Arthur's History of England,' 'Rhymes for Youthful Historians,' and 'Geography,' by 'A Lady.' Butler's 'Gradations' created quite a revolution in the art of teaching to read," &c.

"I don't think he would learn the Church Catechism, but he certainly took his Bible lesson with the others; for I remember a game he joined in with the rest of them one day after they had been reading 'Priests of Baal' in 'Line upon Line.' We heard a curious sort of sing-song in the playground, and, on going to see what it meant, I found that the boys had stuck some clay or mortar on the garden wall, and were crouching down before it in the attitude which had been represented in the picture in the chapter they had read."

EXTRACTS FROM "JOSEPH CHAMBERLAIN: THE MAN AND THE STATESMAN," BY MISS N. MURRELL MARRIS.

(WESTMINSTER GAZETTE, October [illegible])

XLIII.—CAUSE FOR JEALOUSY.

MISS JOSEPHINA: This is dangerous—I must speak to Michael about it.

[At a time when Sir William Harcourt had just been staying with Sir Michael Hicks-Beach, the latter made a speech at Liverpool in which he defended Free Trade principles and severely criticised Mr. Chamberlain's favourite specific, the Imperial Zollverein.]

(WESTMINSTER GAZETTE, October 26, 1903.)

UNIFORM WITH "WESTMINSTER CARTOONS" No. 1.

CARTOONS OF THE CAMPAIGN. By F. C. GOULD.

THIRD EDITION. PRICE ONE SHILLING. By Post 1s. 3d.

THE WESTMINSTER CARTOONS (No. 2).

THE STORY OF THE 1896 SESSION, by F. C. GOULD. POPULAR EDITION, ONE SHILLING.

THE WESTMINSTER CARTOONS

THIRD SERIES

By F. CARRUTHERS GOULD.

THE WESTMINSTER CARTOONS

FOURTH SERIES

A Pictorial History of the South African War in Caricatures

By F. CARRUTHERS GOULD.

PRICE 1d. | POST FREE 1½d.

PICTURE-POLITICS,

A PENNY POPULAR MONTHLY FOR ALL PERSONS INTERESTED IN THE WORK AND WARFARE OF POLITICS OF TO-DAY.

Illustrated and Edited by F. CARRUTHERS GOULD.

CARTOONS, CARICATURES, AND SKETCHES by "F.C.G." POLITICAL EVENTS, DIARY OF THE MONTH, BRIEF ARTICLES, POWDER AND SHOT, NOTES AND SKETCHES IN PARLIAMENT, &c.

SIXTEEN PAGES OF LETTERPRESS AND PICTURES.

A Year's Subscription to PICTURE-POLITICS (Post Free), 1s. 6d.

PICTURE-POLITICS is Full of Points, Full of Pictures, Full of Facts; and, at last, politics are made Pleasant.

"Reading," says Bacon, "maketh a full man, conference a ready man, and writing an exact man."

Read PICTURE-POLITICS, and you will be full of useful facts. Buy it and keep it; read and digest it; and you will be an up-to-date politician.

PICTURE-POLITICS shows the month's political record at a glance.

Members, candidates, and all fighting politicians will find in PICTURE-POLITICS an unfailing supply of Powder and Shot.

Give a copy of PICTURE-POLITICS to your son. He may become a ... some day. Who knows? And the youth of one generation are the electors of the next.

Do not forget the daughters. They will be the "Liberal Women" or Primrose Dames of the future. Influence is as important as votes.

Price One Penny Monthly; by post Eighteenpence a Year. N.B.—Special Terms for Large Quantities. There is no more effective method of Political Education than the distribution of "Picture-Politics."

[illegible]

The Crisis in the Church.

A FULL STATEMENT OF THE CASE.

[illegible]

GIVING IN DETAIL [illegible]

[illegible]

In the Evening of His Days,

BEING A STUDY OF

MR. GLADSTONE IN RETIREMENT.

A CHARMING GIFT-BOOK.

[illegible]

"Who Killed Cock Robin?"

AND OTHER STORIES

By F. C. GOULD.

[illegible]

"The Dolly Dialogues."

By ANTHONY [illegible]

Published at the "WESTMINSTER GAZETTE" Offices: [illegible]

JAEGER

Dr. Jaeger's "HEALTH CULTURE" [illegible]

[illegible]

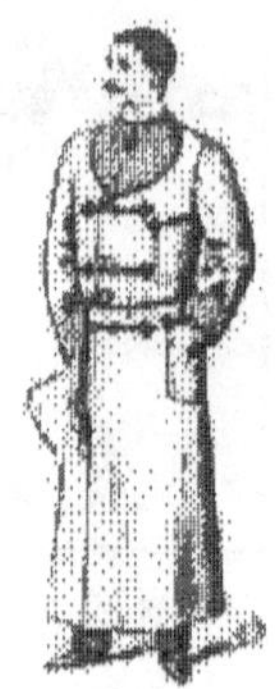

Jaeger Specialty.

MARIANI WINE

THE

BEST AND SUREST

TONIC PICK-ME-UP

SO PLEASANT TO TAKE

So Strengthening & Stimulating for Body and Brain.

[illegible] wineglassfuls daily are [illegible] to work wonders for those suffering from **mental or physical overwork.**

Unsolicited Testimonials have been received from 8,000 Physicians.

FOR GENERAL DEBILITY, EXHAUSTION & WANT OF ENERGY.

His Holiness the Pope [illegible] appreciated the "**beneficent effects of this Tonic Wine**"; and has presented to Mr. Mariani, as a token of his gratitude, a **gold medal** bearing his august **effigy.**

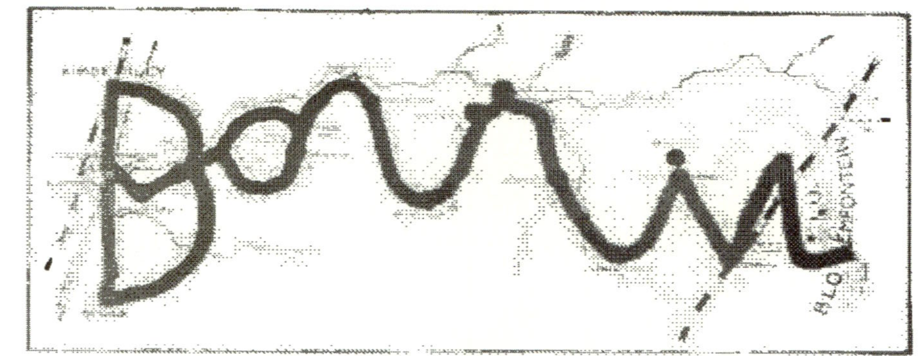

How Lord Roberts wrote BOVRIL

Careful examination of this Map will show that the route followed by Lord Roberts in his historical march to Kimberley and Bloemfontein has made an indelible imprint of the word Bovril on the face of the Orange Free State.

This extraordinary coincidence is one more proof of the universality of Bovril, which has already figured so conspicuously throughout the South African Campaign.

Whether for the Soldier on the Battle field, the Patient in the Sick-room, the Cook in the Kitchen, or for those as yet in full health and strength at home, Bovril is Liquid Life.

Price One Shilling.

THE
WESTMINSTER CARTOONS.

No. 6.—1900 to 1902.

By F. Carruthers Gould.

Published by

THE "WESTMINSTER GAZETTE," Tudor Street, Blackfriars, E.C.

What does it mean?

ONE HUNDRED BRITISH POLICYHOLDERS IN THE M
£1,801,703, an AVERAGE for each of £18,017. One of these insure
has increased from £33,000 to £80,000, while a third has rais
£126,000. In each case the insured draw an immediate income a
annum on the large premiums payable.

The distinctive INVESTMENT advantages offered by the Policies
illustrated by the fact that, of £117,286,370, the total payments m
£63,123,869 has been paid to LIVING POLICYHOLDERS.

"A Policy in THE MUTUAL LIFE not only protects the Family, but is equally valuable a
for the Insured."

TO SECURE THE BEST VALUE FOR MONEY, APPI

THE MUTUAL LIFE INS COM NEW

Established 1843.
RICHARD A. McCURDY, President.

ALL POLICIES now issued by THE MUTUAL LIFE embody conditions of guaranteed AUTOMATIC PAID UP INSURANCE; EXTENDED INSURANCE (Free of further Charge); LOANS; LIBERAL CASH SURRENDER PAYMENTS.

Funds, Nearly £72,000,000.

HEAD OFFICE FOR THE UNITED KINGDOM:

16, 17, & 18, CORNHILL, LONDON, E.C.

D. C. HALDEMAN, General Manager.

INCORPORATED BY ROYAL CHARTER A.D. 1720.

ROYAL EXCHANGE ASSURANCE

Head Office: ROYAL EXCHANGE, LONDON, E.C.

FUNDS IN HAND: (EXPIRED) **£4,600,000**

CLAIMS PAID: (EXCEED) **£40,500,000**

Fire, Life, Sea, Annuities, Accidents, Burglary, Employers' Liability.

PROPOSALS FOR ALL CLASSES OF INSURANCE ARE INVITED.

THE

WESTMINSTER CARTOONS.

VOL. VI.

A Pictorial History of Political Events from the end of 1900 to March, 1902.

BY

F. CARRUTHERS GOULD.

London:
"THE WESTMINSTER GAZETTE," Tudor Street, E.C.

1902.

PREFACE.

The Cartoons which are reproduced in the pages of this volume deal with the principal political events which occurred between the end of 1900, after the General Election in the autumn of that year, and March in the present year 1902.

The first two refer to the reconstruction of Lord Salisbury's Ministry: the Marquis of Lansdowne exchanges the worry of the War Office for the calmer dignity of the Foreign Office, whilst the Cecil family party, consisting of Mr. Arthur Balfour, the Earl of Selborne, Mr. Gerald Balfour and Lord Cranborne walk with or are carried by the head of the House in happy Ministerial ways, leaving Lord Hugh Cecil mourning his isolation.

Next we see Mr. Bull, when well afloat with his boatmen, met with a demand for more money for the war, a war the wearisome prolongation of which is pessimistically suggested by the picture, which follows, of Mr. Chamberlain and Mr. Balfour meeting twenty years hence and discussing the position of De Wet. In the beginning of 1901 we see Lord Roberts installed at the Horse Guards as Commander-in-Chief in succession to Lord Wolseley, and the cartoons "Bobs and the Infant" and "A Real Message from Mars" express the general idea that a great deal of education and sweeping is required to get our military system into better order.

But in spite of Ministerial changes and new brooms the Government continue, apparently, to be as casual as ever. They either slumber, as in Cartoon No. VII., or they think "it really doesn't matter," as in No. VIII., although the relations between Mr. Brodrick, the new Secretary for War, and the new Commander-in-Chief are those of fast and furious harmony (No. IX.), and some of the Ministers regard each other as miracles of successful administration.

The War during the early part of 1901 is the absorbing topic, and the continuity of pictorial comment on its different phases is only broken now and then by the Duke of Devonshire's reminder that the Liberal Unionist Party has not entirely lost its entity, or by Mr.

Chamberlain having once again to disown the Old-Age Pensions foundling. Next we come upon the beginning of the recrudescence of troubles in the Liberal Party. The men in the boat show a disinclination or a disability to pull together, and the distress of the Liberal Party is intensified by the sudden appearance of the Rosebery sea-serpent just when things appeared to be going a little more smoothly. By a Protean change Lord Rosebery is next seen as Robinson Crusoe ploughing a lonely furrow on a desert island. The third year of the War is entered upon and still the Government seem to be drifting as in No. XXI., or harmoniously indifferent as in No. XXV., whilst Mr. Chamberlain still has to wear the same old "fevvers." Cartoon No. XXII. indicates that the Irish question is still alive and may give trouble. Then we have, in November, 1901, Lord Rosebery looking out upon a foggy world from the historic furrow which he has ploughed deep down and emerging at Chesterfield. His suggestion of an "apparently casual meeting in a neutral inn" is illustrated in No. XXIX., and his metaphors of slates and spades have also provided subjects.

With the opening of the Parliamentary Session of 1902 comes the question of remounts. Mr. Balfour considers the old Procedure horse is past his work, and the War Office is haunted and harassed by skeletons of the remounts sent to South Africa.

But there are flashes of brighter things. Mr. Chamberlain goes in triumph to the City, and the Government, forsaking their old love Wei-hai-Wei, form an alliance with the Land of the Chrysanthemum.

In the last four Cartoons we come back to the troubles of the Liberal Party, the slate gets broken, and the definitions lesson is hopelessly bewildering. But, as Cartoon No. XLII. indicates, there is still a possibility that Liberal leaders may chance to meet casually in another wayside Inn, and there find peace.

F. CARRUTHERS GOULD.

CONTENTS.

1.—JONAH—REVISED.

Jonah is cast overboard into the sea, where a Great Fish is kindly prepared to receive him.

The Great Fish maketh Jonah at home and setteth him in a high place.

Lord Lansdowne goes from the War Office to the Foreign Office.

[Westminster Gazette, November 2, 1900.]

11.—ONE THAT WAS LEFT.

Lord Hugh (left behind): Please, mayn't I go too?

III.—MR BULL AND HIS BOATMEN.

BOATMEN: We don't want to hurry you, Gov'nor, but we want more money before we goes any further.
MR. BULL: More money! Why didn't you ask me before I took your boat?
BOATMEN: Well, yo see, Gov'nor, we didn't want you to take t'other boat.

[Parliament is to meet in December. The Times says that there is "not any kind of urgency," but "money will be required before long for the expenses of the war."]

[WESTMINSTER GAZETTE, November 14, 1900.]

IV.—A.D. 1920.

Mr. Chamberlain: Good morning, Arthur, any news? Have they caught De Wet yet?
Mr. Balfour: No, not yet; but I hear he's surrounded.

[Westminster Gazette, [illegible]]

V.—BOBS AND THE INFANT.

"Can't you see I'm busy?"

(With apologies to Mr. Cecil Aldin.)

Westminster Gazette, January 4, 1901.]

VI.—A REAL MESSAGE FROM MARS

"Send me up a brains, please."

[Westminster Gazette, January 10, 1901.

VII.—OUR TSUNGLI YAMÊN

When some Englishmen chaffed a high Chinese official about the ignorance of the Tsungli Yamên he retorted, "You need not speak; you have a Tsungli Yamên of your own in your own Government, who are as blind to their interests as ours are."—A Correspondent.

(Westminster Gazette, January 12, [illegible].)

VIII.—"IT REALLY DOESN'T MATTER!"

A PATTER SONG FOR THE GOVERNMENT CHOIR

[illegible]

[WESTMINSTER GAZETTE, February [illegible].]

IX.—FAST AND FURIOUS—NEW STYLE.

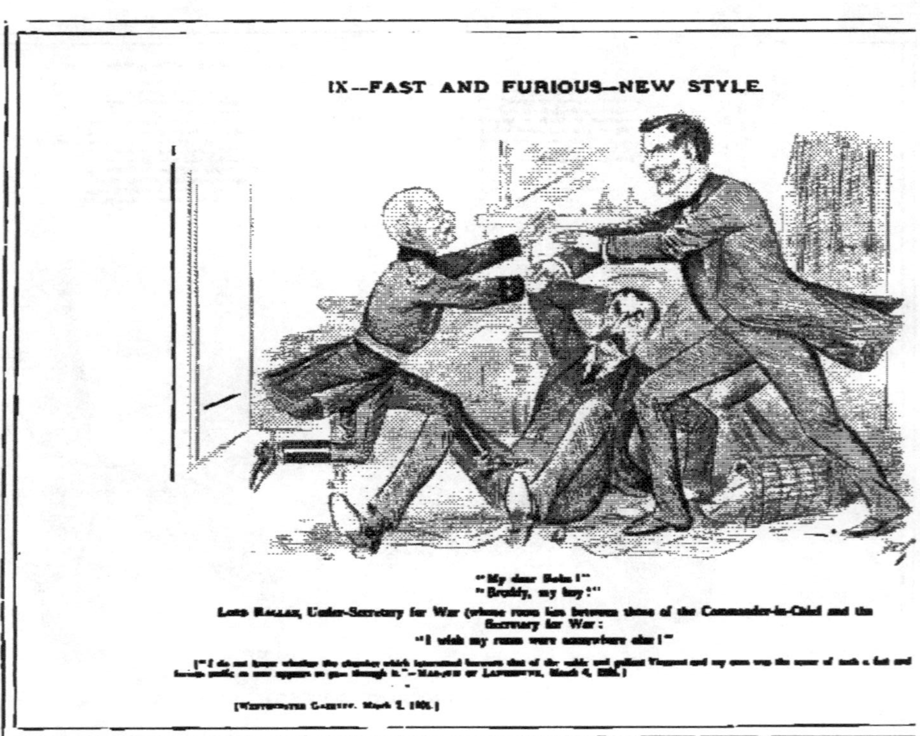

"My dear Bobs!"
"Broddy, my boy!"

LORD RAGLAN, Under-Secretary for War (whose room lies between those of the Commander-in-Chief and the Secretary for War):
"I wish my room were somewhere else!"

["I do not know whether the chamber which intervened between that of the noble and gallant Viscount and my own was the scene of such a fast and furious traffic as now appears to pass through it."—MARQUIS OF LANSDOWNE, March 4, 1901.]

[WESTMINSTER GAZETTE, March [illegible]]

X.—DON'T FORGET THE LITTLE DAWG.

[“No effort should be spared to maintain the vitality and efficiency of the Liberal Unionist Party, and to attach more permanently to our organisation those Liberal electors whose votes were recorded in our favour in the autumn of last year. . . . Mr. Chamberlain cordially concurs in this view.”—Duke of Devonshire's letter to the Liberal Unionist Association, March 1, 1896.]

(Westminster Gazette, March 16, 1896.)

XI.—THE MIRACULOUS BRETHREN.

ADMIRALTY

WAR OFFICE

Maltby (Lord Selborne)
Postlethwaite (Mr. Brodrick) } (simultaneously): Oh, how beautiful! How utterly miraculous!

["Whatever praise they might give to a successful administrator who had a seat in the House of Lords should be given in a far greater measure to a successful administrator in the House of Commons. That Mr. Brodrick was able to administer the Army to the admiration of the Empire under the physical conditions entailed by a seat in the House of Commons was nothing but a miracle."—Lord Selborne, at the Liberal Union Club, March 17, 1901.]

[Westminster Gazette, March [illegible], 1901.]

XII.—COMING HOME TO HIM.

MRS. BULL: Yes, Mr. Bull—sugar's gone up, and treacle's gone up, and jam's gone up, and sweets have gone up, and the blessed children have got to suffer for your foolery. Let me catch you Mafficking again, that's all!

JOHN (pathetically): Don't, my dear; I've got such a headache!

(WESTMINSTER GAZETTE, April 22, 1901.)

XIII.—"WHO SAID BOUNCE?"

Mr. Balfour (wearily): Fancy accusing us of bounce! We don't feel like it, and I'm sure we don't look like it. I feel as limp as a rag.

["Was that our bounce or your bounce?"—Mr. Balfour in the House of Commons, May [illegible]]

[Westminster Gazette, May [illegible]]

XIV.—DEM'D TRIFLING.

MR. JOHN BULL NICKLEBY: What is the gross amount?
MR. "JOE" MANTALINI: Dem'd trifling.

—"NICHOLAS NICKLEBY" (Revised Version).

["We have been called upon, as I say, to make sacrifices. Do not let us exaggerate. When every penny of the new taxation has been paid, the United Kingdom will still be, in proportion to its wealth, the most lightly taxed nation in Europe."—MR. CHAMBERLAIN at Birmingham, May 14, 1894.]

[WESTMINSTER GAZETTE, May 15, 1894.]

XV.—NO "VANITY OF AUTHORSHIP."

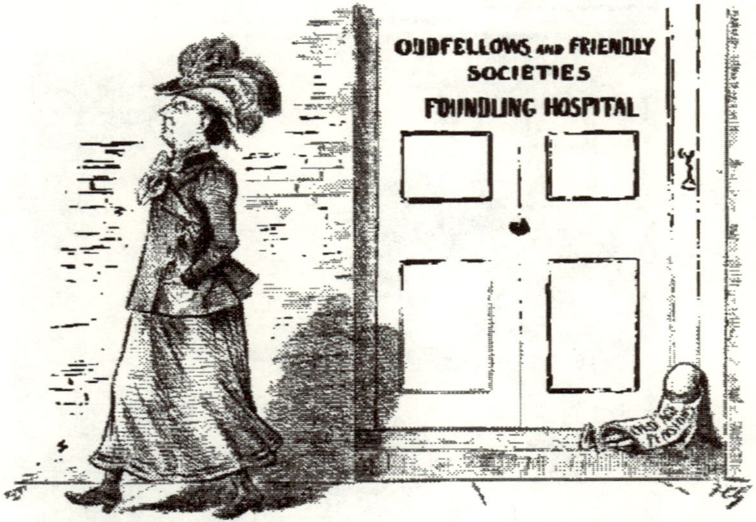

ODDFELLOWS AND FRIENDLY SOCIETIES FOUNDLING HOSPITAL

OLD AGE PENSIONS

"Drat the little wretch, which it ain't mine, and I hate the very name of it. They can take it in there if they like."

["This question of Old-Age Pensions, as it is sometimes called, although that is a description of it which I personally dislike."—"I have put no scheme before you."—"It is desirable that the Friendly Societies, who have already got a larger experience than any one else, who have a greater knowledge of the difficulties of the case, should combine together to form a scheme."—"I want to get rid altogether of the political character of this movement. I have no vanity as an author."—Mr. Chamberlain on Old Age Pensions, at the Annual Conference of Oddfellows, Birmingham, May [illegible].]

[Westminster Gazette, May [illegible].]

XVI.—THE BUSINESS BASIS.

JOHN BULL: I've lost my money.
EX-PRESIDENT KRUGER: I've lost my country.
THE GOLD MINE OWNER: I'm going to lose some of my profits.

[WESTMINSTER GAZETTE, June 17, [illegible].]

XVII.—AN APPEAL.

THE LIBERAL PARTY: Oh, please *do* try and pull together; it's so dreadfully uncomfortable.

(WESTMINSTER GAZETTE, June 12, 1894.)

VIII.—"IT REALLY DOESN'T MATTER!"

A Patter Song for the Government Choir.

[illegible]

[illegible]

[Westminster Gazette, February 18, [illegible].]

IX.—FAST AND FURIOUS—NEW STYLE.

"My dear Bobs!"
"Broddy, my boy!"

Lord Raglan, Under-Secretary for War (whose room lies between those of the Commander-in-Chief and the Secretary for War:

"I wish my room were somewhere else!"

("I do not know whether the chamber which intervened between that of the noble and gallant Viscount and my own was the scene of such a fast and furious traffic as now appears to pass through it."—Marquis of Lansdowne, March 4, 1901.)

[Westminster Gazette, March 7, 1901.]

X.—DON'T FORGET THE LITTLE DAWG.

["[illegible] Liberal Unionist Party, [illegible] Mr. Chamberlain [illegible]"—Duke of Devonshire's letter to the Liberal Unionist Association, March 1, [illegible].]

[Westminster Gazette, March 16, [illegible].]

MAUDLE (Lord Selborne)
POSTLETHWAITE (Mr. Brodrick) } (simultaneously): Oh, how beautiful! How utterly miraculous!

["Whatever praise they might give to a successful administrator who had a seat in the House of Lords should be given in a far greater measure to a successful administrator in the House of Commons. That Mr. Brodrick was able to administer the Army to the admiration of the Empire under the physical consideration entailed by a seat in the House of Commons was nothing but a miracle."—Lord Selborne, at the Liberal Union [illegible], March 22, 190[illegible].]

[Westminster Gazette, March 23, 190[illegible].]

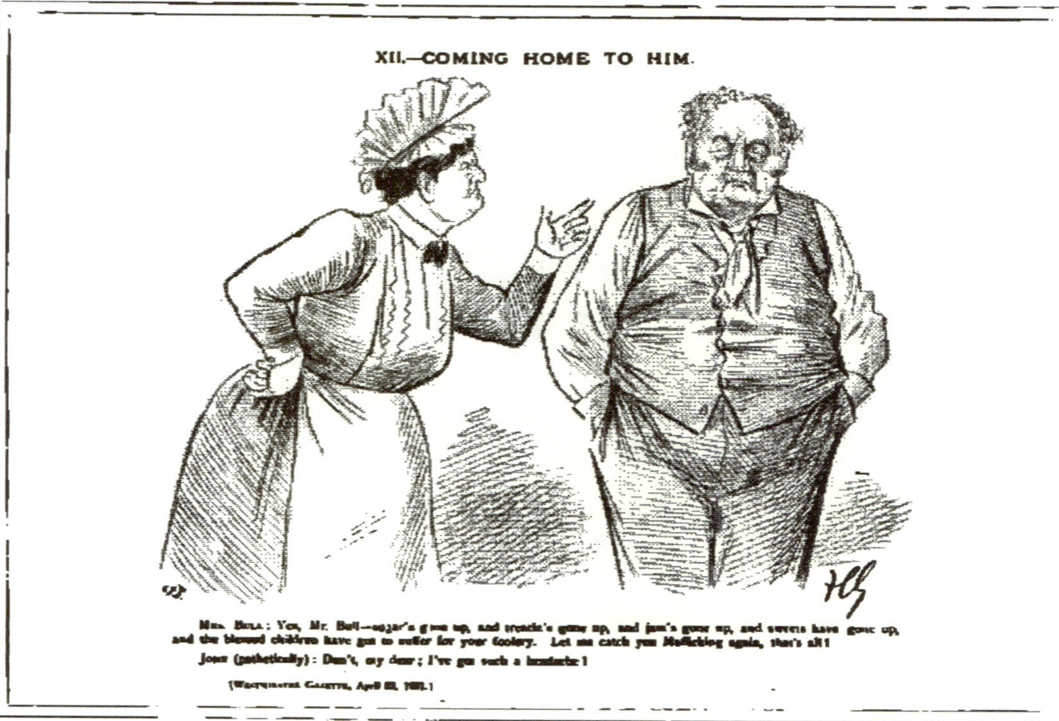

XII.—COMING HOME TO HIM.

MRS. BULL: Yes, Mr. Bull—sugar's gone up, and treacle's gone up, and jam's gone up, and sweets have gone up, and the blessed children have got to suffer for your foolery. Let me catch you Mafficking again, that's all!

JOHN (pathetically): Don't, my dear; I've got such a headache!

[WESTMINSTER GAZETTE, April [illegible], [illegible].]

XIII.—"WHO SAID BOUNCE?"

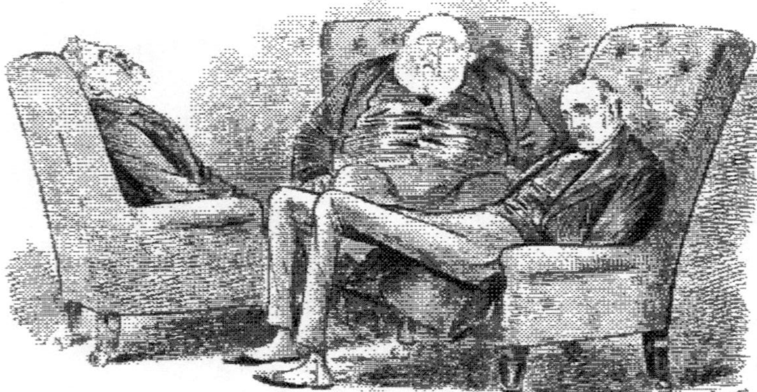

MR. BALFOUR (wearily): Fancy accusing us of bounce! We don't feel like it, and I'm sure we don't look like it. I feel as limp as a rag.

["Was that our bounce or your bounce?"—MR. BALFOUR in the House of Commons, May [illegible], 1893.]

[WESTMINSTER GAZETTE, May [illegible], 1893.]

XIV.—DEM'D TRIFLING.

Mr. John Bull Nickleby: What is the gross amount?

Mr. "Joe" Mantalini: Dem'd trifling.

"Nicholas Nickleby" (Revised Version).

["We have been called upon, as I say, to make sacrifices. Do not let us exaggerate. When every penny of the new taxation has been paid, the United Kingdom will still be, in proportion to its wealth, the most lightly taxed nation in Europe."—Mr. Chamberlain at Birmingham, May 16, 1902.]

[Westminster Gazette, May 1[illegible], [illegible].]

XV.—NO "VANITY OF AUTHORSHIP."

"Drat the little wretch, which it ain't mine, and I hate the very name of it. They can take it in there if they like."

["This question of Old-Age Pensions, as it is sometimes called, although that is a description of it which I personally dislike"——"I have put the scheme before you"——"It is desirable that the Friendly Societies, who have already got a larger experience than any one else, who have a greater knowledge of the difficulties of the case, should consider together to form a scheme"——"I want to get rid altogether of the political character of this movement. I have no vanity as an author."—Mr. Chamberlain on Old-Age Pensions, at the Annual Conference of Oddfellows, Birmingham, May 20, 1896.]

[Westminster Gazette, May 22, 1896.]

XVI.—THE BUSINESS BASIS.

JOHN BULL: I've lost my money.
EX-PRESIDENT KRUGER: I've lost my country.
THE GOLD MINE OWNER: I'm going to lose some of my profits.

[WESTMINSTER GAZETTE, June 12, 1901.]

XVII.—AN APPEAL.

THE LIBERAL PARTY: Oh, please do try and pull together; it's so dreadfully uncomfortable.

[Westminster Gazette, June 22, 1893.]

XVIII.—MORE HORRIBLE EXAMPLES.

THE DOOK: Just think wot these awful Liberals are a-wanting ter do! Why, they wants to disestablish the Church and the 'Ouse o' Lords and ter rob the pore man of his beer, and ter start 'Ome Rule and Universal School Boards!

JOE (groaning as the memory of his Unauthorised Programme is borne in upon him): Wot awful depravity!

["If any of those who were present were thinking of transferring their votes and influence to the Liberal Party, who, he thought there was reason to doubt, were returned on Tuesday, he asked them to consider what was the policy to which they would find themselves pledged in the new Parliament. They would be committed to Home Rule for Ireland, and perhaps for Scotland and Wales also; they would be committed to the disestablishment of the House of Lords; they would be pledging themselves to the disestablishment of the Church in Wales as a preparation to the disestablishment of the Church of England; they would be pledging themselves to give to a majority in any parish, or perhaps to an active minority, the power to impose compulsory abstinence from liquor; they would be pledging themselves to the establishment of Universal School Boards and the withdrawal of all State aid from denominational schools."—THE DUKE OF DEVONSHIRE, at the Liberal Unionist dinner, July 20, 18[illegible].]

[WESTMINSTER GAZETTE, July 1[illegible], 18[illegible]

XIX.—ANOTHER SHOCK

LIBERAL PARTY: Oh, deary me! What's the trouble now? And just when we were beginning to get on again so nicely, too!

THE SEA-SERPENT: Don't be frightened, ma'am; I've only come up to Blow

["I hold myself absolutely free from the restraint which I have imposed upon myself nearly five years ago. But that I desire to re-enter the arena of party politics; far from it. I shall never voluntarily return to it."—LORD ROSEBERY'S letter to the City Liberal Club.]

(WESTMINSTER GAZETTE, July 13, 1901.)

XX.—THE LONE, LONG FURROW.

"I must plough my furrow alone. That is my fate, agreeable or the reverse, but before I get to the end of the furrow it is possible that I may find myself not alone."

—Lord Rosebery, at the City Liberal Club, July 19, 1901.

Mr. Gibson Bowles in the House of Commons quoted apropos of Lord Rosebery's position, from Cowper's lines on Alexander Selkirk.

I am out of humanity's reach,
I must finish my journey alone,
Never hear the sweet music of speech,
I start at the sound of my own.

[Westminster Gazette, July 20, 1901.]

XXI.—DRIFTING WITH THE TIDE.

The jelly fish is a marine animal, gelatinous and free-swimming. It has thread-cells, or urticating organs, which, by discharging minute barbed structures, cause irritation on contact.

["Who are we that we should attempt to stem the tide? If the tide has turned we shall have to go with it."—Lord Salisbury, on the [illegible] Bill, in the House of Lords, July [illegible].]

[Westminster Gazette, July [illegible].]

XXII.—TAIL AND CLAWS.

ARTHUR B.: I say, Joe, here's the cat that's always making such a horrid noise.
JOE: Let's cut a bit off his tail!
THE CAT: You may cut my tail, but you can't cut my claws.

["The [illegible] in the country would be [illegible] to the Government if the representation was reduced."—Mr. John Redmond, at [illegible], September 1, 1901.] [Westminster Gazette, September [illegible], 1901.]

XXIII.—ON THE LINKS OF EMPIRE

MR. ASQUITH: I say, Arthur, the war news isn't very satisfactory.

MR. BALFOUR: What war? The South African? Why, I thought that was finished on September 15. We fixed the date!

[WESTMINSTER GAZETTE, September [illegible].]

XXIV.—TO BE CLEARED OUT.

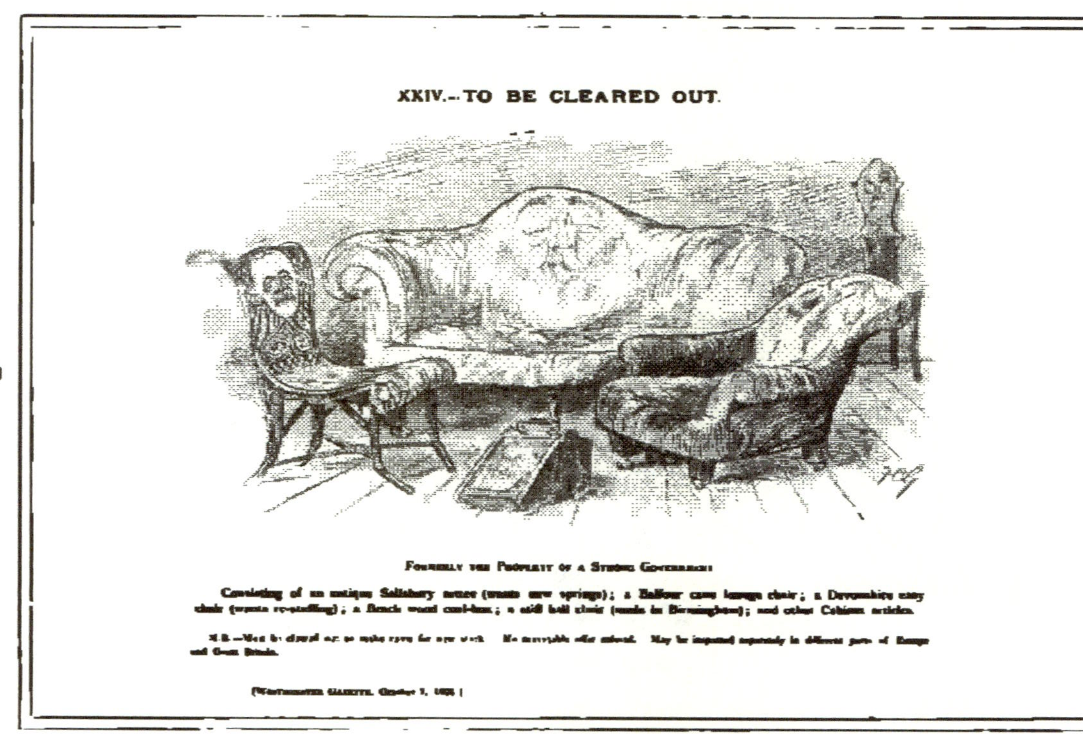

FORMERLY THE PROPERTY OF A STRONG GOVERNMENT

Consisting of an antique Salisbury settee (wants new springs); a Balfour cane lounge chair; a Devonshire easy chair (wants re-stuffing); a Beach wood coal-box; a stiff hall chair (made in Birmingham); and other Cabinet articles.

N.B.—Must be cleared out to make room for new stock. No reasonable offer refused. May be inspected separately in different parts of Europe and Great Britain.

[WESTMINSTER GAZETTE, October [illegible].]

XXV.—OUR PIERROTS.

We don't want to fight,
But by jingo when we do,
We're reckless and we're misinformed
And optimistic too.

We can't conduct a *War*,
We won't arrange a *Peace*,
So we don't know when the fighting
will be over.

["What were they to say of the authors of the documents to which he had called their attention? They would always stand as masterpieces in the history of reckless and misinformed optimism."—Mr. Asquith in East Fife, September 28, 1901.]

[Westminster Gazette, October 8, 1901.]

XXVI.—BY THE SHORE OF A TIDELESS SEA.

LORD S.: What I particularly like about this Mediterranean sea is its beautiful tidelessness. No worry about either stemming or drifting.

[Holding the views he does about the formidable nature of tides, Lord Salisbury naturally takes his holidays on the shores of a tideless sea. As he said in his speech in the House of Lords, July [illegible], [illegible]:

"Who are we that we should attempt to stem the tide? If the tide has turned, we shall have to go with it."]

[WESTMINSTER GAZETTE, October 7, [illegible].]

XXVII.—THE OLD FEATHERS.

"It's 'ard luck I've got to wear the same old feevers three years runnin'."

(The war, which Mr. Chamberlain once said would be a feather in his cap were he responsible for it, has now entered upon its third year.)

[Westminster Gazette, October 16, 1901.]

XXVIII.—COMING OUT.

LORD R.: It's awfully dull down here. I think I *must* get out and see what's going on up above. Humph! A little foggy!

[WESTMINSTER GAZETTE, November 6, 1901.]

XXIX.—APPARENTLY CASUAL

JOE: Why, dang me if it bain't Mr. Kruger—who'd a' thought it? I'd a' knawed ee anywhere!
KRUGER: To be sure now! if it bain't Joe! Yew bain't changed a bit!
JOE: Only to fancy us meetin' casual like and in the same public-'ouse too!
KRUGER: It's a Hact o' Providence, it is—an' nothin' else!

["Some of the greatest peaces, the greatest settlements in the world's history, have begun in an apparently casual meeting in a neutral inn." —LORD ROSEBERY, at Chesterfield, December 16, 1901.]

[WESTMINSTER GAZETTE, December 18, 1901.]

XXX.—LOOKING OUT ON THE NEW YEAR.

"How about the other poultry? Shall I join them, or will they call on me?"

[Westminster Gazette, January 1, [illegible].]

XXXI.—ON THE WAVE

A clean slate and a flowing speech,
And a spade that follows free

[Westminster Gazette, January 3, 1902.]

XXXII.—CONSOLATION.

Mr. C. (apostrophising portrait of William Pitt): It's wonderful, William, how much alike all we great Ministers are. You were hated in Europe in your time as I am hated to-day.

["Read your history, and you find the younger Pitt, one of the greatest of English Ministers; you find Lord Melbourne, you find the Duke of Wellington, you find Lord Palmerston—you find all these great Ministers who in their time upheld the honour and interests of the British Empire—you find them all complaining that they had not a friend in Europe . . . . sometimes that it is a consolation to me."—Mr. Chamberlain at Birmingham, January 6, 1902.]

[Westminster Gazette, January 8, 1902.]

XXXIII.—SPADE WORK.

NURSE C.-B.: Now then, Edward and George, take a spade each of you, like good little boys, and go and work all together in the garden.

FIRST BOY: I don't mind taking a spade, but I'm not going to dig with some of these other boys.

SECOND BOY: I won't dig unless I can dig where I like.

[*Westminster Gazette*, January [illegible].]

XXXIV.—THAT OLD HORSE.

MR. BULL: Well, Arthur, how does the old horse carry you?

MR. BALFOUR: Very badly; he's a regular old crock. I can't do anything with him.

MR. BULL: Humph! You both of you want a tonic.

(WESTMINSTER GAZETTE, January [illegible].)

XXXV.—EGGS AND EGGS.

A New Application of the Old "Curate's Egg" Story.

Bishop: I'm afraid that egg is not quite to your liking.

Curate: I assure you, my lord, it's excellent—*in parts*.

("There are eggs and eggs."—Sir William Harcourt at the meeting of the National Poultry Organisation Society, February 4, 1903.)

[Westminster Gazette, February 6, 1903.]

XXXVI.—A SORT OF A REMOUNT SYSTEM.

SOME EXPENSIVE STUDIES IN ANATOMY.

(Dedicated to the War Office.)

(WESTMINSTER GAZETTE, February [illegible], 1902.)

XXXVII—SIC TRANSIT GLORIA—THURSDAY.

Mr. Chamberlain Visited the City in State on Thursday, February 13

XXXVIII.—AN EASTERN ENTANGLEMENT

Mr. Bull (A.B.): Wei-hai-Wei! Don't you be jealous. I ain't going back there again. I'm going to stick to you now. Why shouldn't I have a sweetheart in every port? Blow the consequences

Russia: I wonder what he's up to now?

[Westminster Gazette, February 14, 1902.]

XXXIX.—A MAN OF THESSALY

There was a man of Thessaly,
And he was wondrous wise;
He jumped into a quickset hedge
And badly scratched his Ayes.

Now, when he saw his Ayes were hurt,
He roared with might and main,
And jumped into another hedge
To scratch them well again.

[Westminster Gazette, February [illegible], [illegible].]

XL.—THAT SLATE.

Liberal Party: What are you doing with that slate?
Boys: We're discussing whether we shall clean it or not.
Liberal Party: You'll break it in pieces between you if you don't take care.

[Westminster Gazette, February 16, 1893.]

XLI.—CLEAN BUT BROKEN.

SIR H. C.-B. : Well, this isn't much use without the other

LORD R. : Nor's this

XLII.—WANTED—ANOTHER WAYSIDE INN.

Eh! man, it's just a meeracle meetin' ye here—dod! I've clean forgotten what a' our havers were about.
Was it no the roofin' o' the Tabernacle? Ye wanted the auld thatch and I wanted the clean slates.
Oh ay! I mind it noo—we fairly dinged the congregation oot between us.

[Westminster Gazette, February [illegible].]

XLIII.—DEFINITIONS.

Q. What is a "Party"?
A. A number of people who don't agree with each other. It is derived from the verb "to part" or to separate.
Q. What is "Party Feeling"?
A. The feeling you have towards members of your own party.
Q. What is a "Tabernacle"?
A. A sort of a (Dissent) Tent.
Q. What is a "State"?
A. A thing that splits easily into thin sections.
Q. What is a "Phylactery"?
A. A thing that somebody else wears.
Q. What are "Cross-Currents"?
A. Currents produced by people when they are cross.
Q. What, then, is the "Main Stream"?
A. The particular cross-current in which the swimmer finds himself.
Q. What is "Spade-work"?
A. Turning things upside down.
Q. What is a "Metaphor"?
A. A sort of a boomerang.

[Westminster Gazette, February 9th, 1898.]

www.ingramcontent.com/pod-product-compliance
Lightning Source LLC
Chambersburg PA
CBHW030808230426
43667CB00008B/1123

* 9 7 8 3 7 4 1 1 9 5 7 6 1 *